FORMED IN C

MW00850050

ABOUT THE SERIES

Who is Jesus Christ? What does it mean to know him? What do the Church and her sacraments have to do with him? How are we to follow him?

These are the questions at the heart of the Catholic faith, and these are the questions the Formed in Christ series answers. Rooted in the story of Salvation History and steeped in the writings of the Fathers and Doctors of the Church, this series of high school textbooks from the St. Paul Center seeks to engage minds and hearts as it presents the tenets of the Catholic faith in Scripture and Tradition.

Over the course of this comprehensive, four-year curriculum, students will learn the fundamentals of Church teaching on the Person and mission of Jesus Christ, Sacred Scripture, the Church, the sacraments, morality, Church history, vocations, Catholic social teaching, and more. Just as important, they'll be invited, again and again, to enter more deeply into a relationship with Christ, growing in love of him as they grow in knowledge of him.

PUBLISHED

Evidence of Things Unseen: An Introduction to Fundamental Theology
Andrew Willard Jones and Louis St. Hilaire.
Edited by Emily Stimpson Chapman

The Word Became Flesh: An Introduction to Christology
Andrew Willard Jones. Edited by Emily Stimpson Chapman

That You Might Have Life: An Introduction to the Paschal Mystery of Christ
Louis St. Hilaire. Edited by Emily Stimpson Chapman

I Will Build My Church: An Introduction to Ecclesiology
Andrew Willard Jones. Edited by Emily Stimpson Chapman

Do This in Remembrance: An Introduction to the Sacraments
Jacob Wood. Edited by Emily Stimpson Chapman

Christ Alive in Us: An Introduction to Moral Theology
John Meinert and Emily Stimpson Chapman

I HAVE CALLED YOU

An Introduction to Vocations

I HAVE CALLED YOU

AN INTRODUCTION TO VOCATIONS

EMILY STIMPSON CHAPMAN

TAN Books &
Emmaus Road Publishing

In Grateful Recognition of Lawrence Joseph & Lynn Marie Blanford

Cover image: St. Peter Invited to Walk on the Water, 1766, Francois Boucher. National Trust Photographic Library / John Hammond / Bridgeman Images.

Series design by Margaret Ryland

ISBN 978-1-5051-2068-4

Emmaus Road Publishing
1468 Parkview Circle
Steubenville, Ohio 43952

TAN Books
PO Box 269
Gastonia, NC 28053

Printed in the United States of America

TABLE OF CONTENTS

Part I

GOD'S CALL TO EACH OF US

"Before I formed you in the womb, I knew you" (Jer 1:5). Before the world existed—before the sun shone in the sky, before the fish swam in oceans or flowers bloomed in spring—God knew you would exist. He knew every part of you. He knew what you would look like: the color of your hair, the shape of your nose, and how tall you would grow. He also knew who you would be: what you would love and what you would find interesting, what things would make you happy and what things would make you sad. He knew every strength and virtue that would come naturally to you and knew how you would struggle as your life unfolded. He knew your good deeds before you performed them and your sins before you committed them.

There is no part of you that has ever or will ever be hidden from God. He saw everything about you from all eternity—all the gifts he would give you and all the ways you would use and misuse those gifts—and he loved you just the same. That's why you exist. Because God loves you. He loved you into existence and his love continues to hold you in existence. His being sustains your being and his grace surrounds you, offering you help in every moment of the day. God is as interested and as involved in your life now as he was at the moment he created you. Nothing that you have done in all the intervening years has changed that, and nothing ever will.

This means that no matter how uninterested in God you've felt, no matter how angry you might have been at him, no matter how much you ignored him, disobeyed him, or rejected him, he has not abandoned you. He has a plan just for you—a plan that will fulfill you and bring you joy for all eternity. He wants you to know that plan, and he wants you to say yes to it.

That's what this book is about: God's plan for your life—his call to you. The word the Church uses to describe this call is "vocation," and in the following chapters we're going to talk about what that word means, the different types of vocations that exist, and how you can discern the vocation to which God is calling you.

Chapter 1

The Universal Call to Holiness

When talking about vocations, it's important to keep in mind that you have more than one "vocation." There are many different types of "calls" from God that you will hear over the course of your life, and those calls won't necessarily be the same as the calls God issues to everyone else. There is one call that everyone does share, though: the universal vocation to holiness.

God calls every single man and woman to holiness—he calls all of us to become saints. Quoting the Second Vatican Council document *Lumen Gentium* and Sacred Scripture, the Catechism of the Catholic Church states: "'All Christians in any state or walk of life are called to the fullness of Christian life and to the perfection of charity' [LG 40 §2]. All are called to holiness: 'Be perfect, as your Heavenly Father is perfect' [Matt 5:48]" (CCC 2013).

That sounds like a tall order, doesn't it? How can God expect you to become a saint, let alone "perfect" as he is perfect? It's true; the vocation to holiness is not an easy call to answer. But it's also what you were made for. Holy is what you were created to be.

A Communion of Love

God, remember, is a Holy Trinity. He is three divine Persons sharing one divine nature, and that nature is self-giving love. God can't help but give himself away in love. That's who he is. It's what he has been doing from all eternity. God the Father pours out to God the Son everything he has and is. God the Son, in turn, receives all that the Father has to give and then gives it right back. The Father holds nothing back from the Son, and the Son holds nothing back from the Father. Because of that, the exchange between them is so real and so complete that it too is a Person, the Holy Spirit, the Third Person of the Trinity.

But it wasn't enough for God to keep that exchange of love within the Trinity. Again, that's not who he is. God wants to share his love and share his life; he doesn't want to contain it. His love spills over into every corner of the universe. Pope Benedict XVI writes:

> God is wholly and only love, the purest, infinite and eternal love. He does not live in splendid solitude but rather is an inexhaustible source of life that is ceaselessly given and communicated. To a certain extent we can perceive this by observing both the macro-universe: our earth, the planets, the stars, the galaxies; and the micro-universe: cells, atoms, elementary particles. The "name" of the Blessed Trinity is, in a certain sense, imprinted upon all things because all that exists, down to the last particle, is in relation; in this way we catch a glimpse of God as relationship and ultimately, Creator Love. All things derive from love, aspire to love and move impelled by love, though naturally with varying degrees of awareness and freedom.[1]

Most importantly, God's love spills over into us. God created us out of love and for love, and that is reflected in every part of who we are. As

---

[1] Pope Benedict XVI, Sunday Angelus (June 7, 2009), available from http://w2.vatican.va/content/benedict-xvi/en/angelus/2009/documents/hf_ben-xvi_ang_20090607.html.

the Bible says, we are made in his image (Gen 1:27). This means, in part, that we have the ability to reason and freely choose right from wrong. We can use our reason and free will to make things, build things, and grow things, to think through tough problems and find good solutions, all in imitation of the One who created all things and knows all things.

Being made in God's image also means we have the ability to give ourselves away in love. We can make a gift of who we are—our time, our talents, our affections, our intellect, and our bodies—to help others and serve others. When we give ourselves away in love, our love becomes life-giving, whether spiritually (helping people find wisdom, hope, encouragement, compassion, truth, beauty, or goodness) or physically (creating new life through the marital act).

For this reason, Pope St. John Paul II could write in his *Theology of the Body*, "Man becomes the image of God not so much in the moment of solitude as in the moment of communion."[2] Or, as he states in *Familiaris Consortio*, "Love is . . . the fundamental and innate vocation of every human being."[3]

In other words, God created us to share in his love, to love one another, and to love him. That's the life to which God calls us: he calls us to participate in the eternal communion of life and love that is the Trinity.

Holiness is nothing more and nothing less than answering that call. It is saying no to all the things that pull us away from God—selfishness, hatred, lies, cruelty, wrath, envy, lust, resentment, and greed—and saying yes to all the things that draw us closer to him—humility, gentleness, wisdom, chastity, peace, kindness, honesty, compassion, mercy, and forgiveness. Holiness is seeking God before all other things and above all other things. It also is seeking to love others and treat them as the images of God that they are—never using other people for our own selfish purposes, never intentionally harming them in body or soul, never belittling or demeaning anyone, but always respecting, honoring, and helping people to become who God made them to be.

---

[2] Pope John Paul II, The Redemption of the Body and Sacramentality of Marriage (Theology of the Body) (September 5, 1979–November 28, 1984), 9:3.

[3] Pope John II, Apostolic Exhortation on the Role of the Christian Family in the Modern World *Familiaris Consortio* (November 22, 1981), §11.

The Way of Discipleship

|| **ASSIGNED READING**
|| Matthew 6:9–13

Deep, abiding, faithful love, love that sees, knows, and honors us, love that is divine, is the deepest desire of our hearts. It is that love for which we long. But in this fallen world we often seek it in the wrong ways and the wrong places. We think that money or things, success or power, sex or fame will bring us the love we desire. And so we chase after those things. When we get the things we were chasing, though, we always find it's not enough. They don't satisfy us like we thought they would. They can't.

No matter how much money, fame, or power we attain, no matter our accomplishments, no matter how many romantic partners we have, no matter how many things we acquire, none of it can make us truly happy— not in a lasting way. Finite goods can't fill the infinite hole in our hearts that can be filled by God alone. God made us for himself, and so, ultimately, nothing less than God will do. To paraphrase St. Augustine, our hearts will always be restless until they rest in God.[4]

Recognizing this is the first step towards holiness. When we realize we were made for a love far greater than any earthly love, we can start out on the path that God has laid out for us—the path to himself. This path is the way of discipleship, and Jesus Christ himself showed us how we are to walk this path.

Obedience to God

First, if we wish to be disciples, we must obey God, starting with the Commandments. "If you love me," Jesus says in John 14:15, "you will keep my commandments." These commandments include the Ten Commandments given by God to the Israelites, the Beatitudes preached by Jesus in the Sermon on the Mount (Matt 5–7), and what Jesus called "the two

---

[4] St. Augustine, *The Confessions*, 1.1.1.

greatest Commandments," which sum up all the laws and teachings of Sacred Scripture:

> You shall love the Lord your God with all your heart, and with all your soul, and with all your mind. This is the great and first commandment. And a second is like it, You shall love your neighbor as yourself. (Matt 22:37–39)

Obedience to God also includes following Jesus' instructions to care for the poor, the hungry, the naked, the imprisoned, the sick, the dying, the widowed, the orphaned, the stranger, and the ignorant. These are what the Church calls the corporal works of mercy, and she has always understood that when we are caring for others, we are caring for Jesus himself.

> Then the King will say to those at his right hand, "Come, O blessed of my Father, inherit the kingdom prepared for you from the foundation of the world; for I was hungry and you gave me food, I was thirsty and you gave me drink, I was a stranger and you welcomed me, I was naked and you clothed me, I was sick and you visited me, I was in prison and you came to me." Then the righteous will answer him, "Lord, when did we see you hungry and feed you, or thirsty and give you drink? And when did we see you a stranger and welcome you, or naked and clothe you? And when did we see you sick or in prison and visit you?" And the King will answer them, "Truly, I say to you, as you did it to one of the least of these my brethren, you did it to me." (Matt 25:34–40)

The last thing obedience requires is sharing the Good News of Jesus Christ. "You are the light of the world," he told his followers in the Sermon on the Mount. "Let your light so shine before men, that they may see your good works and give glory to your Father who is in heaven"(Matt 5:14, 16). Later, before his Ascension into heaven, he instructed his disciples, "Go therefore and make disciples of all nations" (Matt 28:19).

Carrying the Cross

In addition to obedience, discipleship also means sharing in Jesus' suffering. "And he called to him the multitude with his disciples, and said to them, 'If any man would come after me, let him deny himself and take up his cross and follow me'" (Mark 8:34).

Part of carrying our cross is dying to ourselves—letting go of all our desires and dreams that are not in line with God's will for us so that we can pursue all that God does will. Jesus tells us this in Matthew 16:25: "For whoever would save his life will lose it, and whoever loses his life for my sake will find it."

Carrying our cross also entails a willingness to sacrifice for the good of another: "By this we know love, that he laid down his life for us; and we ought to lay down our lives for the brethren" (1 John 3:16).

And carrying our cross entails bearing with patience, faith, hope, and love all the ordinary and extraordinary trials that come our way in life, for as we're told in the Epistle of James, "Blessed is the man who endures trial, for when he has stood the test he will receive the crown of life which God has promised to those who love him" (Jas 1:12).

A Life of Prayer

Along with obedience and carrying our cross, discipleship requires prayer. This prayer follows the pattern given to us by Jesus:

> Our Father who art in Heaven,
> Hallowed be thy name.
> Thy kingdom come.
> Thy will be done,
> On earth as it is in Heaven.
> Give us this day our daily bread;
> And forgive us our trespasses,
> As we forgive those who trespass against us;
> And lead us not into temptation,
> But deliver us from evil. (Matt 6:9–13)

In other words, when we pray, we are to approach God as a loving Father who desires the best for us. We are to place our needs before him, trusting in his will. We also are to confess our sins to him, asking for his forgiveness. And we are to beg him for protection and guidance as we face the temptations of this world.

The Sacramental Life

Lastly, walking the way of discipleship means accepting all the helps God gives us in the sacraments. So we must be baptized: "Truly, truly, I say to you, unless one is born of water and the Spirit, he cannot enter the kingdom of God" (John 3:5). We must "receive the Holy Spirit" in Confirmation (John 20:22) and "confess our sins" in the Sacrament of Reconciliation (1 John 1:9; Jas 5:16). We also must receive the Eucharist.

> So Jesus said to them, "Truly, truly, I say to you, unless you eat the flesh of the Son of man and drink his blood, you have no life in you; he who eats my flesh and drinks my blood has eternal life, and I will raise him up at the last day. For my flesh is food indeed, and my blood is drink indeed. He who eats my flesh and drinks my blood abides in me, and I in him. As the living Father sent me, and I live because of the Father, so he who eats me will live because of me." (John 6:53–57)

Through obedience, suffering, prayer, and the reception of the sacraments we walk the path of discipleship. And as we do, God sanctifies us. He makes us holy, supplying us with the graces we need to follow him, obey him, and become more and more like him every day.

SELECTED READING
Second Vatican Council, Dogmatic Constitution on the Church *Lumen Gentium* (November 21, 1964), no. 42

"God is love, and he who abides in love, abides in God and God in

Him." But, God pours out his love into our hearts through the Holy Spirit, Who has been given to us; thus the first and most necessary gift is love, by which we love God above all things and our neighbor because of God. Indeed, in order that love, as good seed may grow and bring forth fruit in the soul, each one of the faithful must willingly hear the Word of God and accept His Will, and must complete what God has begun by their own actions with the help of God's grace. These actions consist in the use of the sacraments and in a special way the Eucharist, frequent participation in the sacred action of the Liturgy, application of oneself to prayer, self-abnegation, lively fraternal service and the constant exercise of all the virtues. For charity, as the bond of perfection and the fullness of the law, rules over all the means of attaining holiness and gives life to these same means. It is charity which guides us to our final end. It is the love of God and the love of one's neighbor which points out the true disciple of Christ.

Since Jesus, the Son of God, manifested His charity by laying down His life for us, so too no one has greater love than he who lays down his life for Christ and His brothers. From the earliest times, then, some Christians have been called upon—and some will always be called upon—to give the supreme testimony of this love to all men, but especially to persecutors. The Church, then, considers martyrdom as an exceptional gift and as the fullest proof of love. By martyrdom a disciple is transformed into an image of his Master by freely accepting death for the salvation of the world—as well as his conformity to Christ in the shedding of his blood. Though few are presented such an opportunity, nevertheless all must be prepared to confess Christ before men. They must be prepared to make this profession of faith even in the midst of persecutions, which will never be lacking to the Church, in following the way of the cross.

Likewise, the holiness of the Church is fostered in a special way by the observance of the counsels proposed in the Gospel by Our Lord to His disciples. An eminent position among these is held by virginity or the celibate state. This is a precious gift of divine grace given by the Father to certain souls, whereby they may devote themselves to God alone the more easily, due to an undivided heart. This perfect continency, out of desire for the kingdom of heaven, has always been held in particular honor in the Church. The reason for this was and is that perfect continency for the love of God is an incentive to charity, and is certainly a particular source of spiritual fecundity in the world.

The Church continually keeps before it the warning of the Apostle which moved the faithful to charity, exhorting them to experience personally what Christ Jesus had known within Himself. This was the same Christ Jesus, who "emptied Himself, taking the nature of a slave . . . becoming obedient to death," and because of us "being rich, he became poor." Because the disciples must always offer an imitation of and a testimony to the charity and humility of Christ, Mother Church rejoices at finding within her bosom men and women who very closely follow their Saviour who debased Himself to our comprehension. There are some who, in their freedom as sons of God, renounce their own wills and take upon themselves the state of poverty. Still further, some become subject of their own accord to another man, in the matter of perfection for love of God. This is beyond the measure of the commandments, but is done in order to become more fully like the obedient Christ.

Therefore, all the faithful of Christ are invited to strive for the holiness and perfection of their own proper state. Indeed they have an obligation to so strive. Let all then have care that they guide aright their own deepest sentiments of soul. Let neither the use of the things of this world nor attachment to riches, which is against the spirit of evangelical poverty, hinder them in their quest for perfect love. Let them heed the admonition of the Apostle to those who use this world; let them not come to terms with this world; for this world, as we see it, is passing away.

QUESTIONS FOR REVIEW

1. To what vocation does God call every single human person?
2. What are the three primary ways in which men and women "image God"?
3. For what three purposes did God create us?
4. What are the four basic elements to discipleship?
5. What prayer is the model for all prayer?

QUESTIONS FOR DISCUSSION

1. Have you ever met someone you would characterize as holy? Describe that person.
2. Who is someone you know that has "carried their cross" well? What did they do? How did that inspire you?
3. How would you describe your prayer life? Is it easy for you to talk to God or difficult? How often do you talk to him? What do you talk about? How would you like to see your prayer life grow or change?

Chapter 2

The Personal Call

Holiness is the call God issues to each and every one of us. Answering that call requires following the path he has laid out for us: the path of discipleship. But as we walk that path God calls to us in different and more personal ways.

Particular Vocations

Some of those calls will be determined by your age, state in life, interests, abilities, and opportunities. For example, right now you have a "vocation" to be a student. Eventually, you will have a "vocation" to work in a particular place at a particular job. Maybe you have a vocation to be a writer or a teacher, a doctor or a lawyer, a public servant or a small business owner.

These vocations, which are all part of the vocations of Catholics who are not ordained or consecrated, are sometimes referred to as "occupational vocations," "secondary vocations," or "particular vocations." It's important to understand that they're much more than a job or a career. They are a way of serving God and others in the world and, through that service, growing in holiness.

God has equipped each of us for a particular task. Perhaps he has given you a mind that is unusually good at understanding how the human body works, sharp eyes, and steady hands. Those gifts could be signs that

God is calling you to serve others as a surgeon. Or maybe you have a gift for writing and a great love for the Church. The combination of your gifts and interests could mean that God will call you to be a theologian or a Catholic writer.

Whatever your gifts, talents, and interests are, they have been given to you for a purpose. The world needs men and women who care about more than simply making money and acquiring power. It needs people who are committed to serving God and the common good through their work; who see what they do from nine to five as a way of glorifying God and helping others; who work with integrity and never forget that every person they encounter through their work—their coworkers, clients, customers, patients, shareholders, or readers—is someone who is made in the image of God. The Catechism states:

> "By reason of their special vocation it belongs to the laity to seek the kingdom of God by engaging in temporal affairs and directing them according to God's will. . . . It pertains to them in a special way so to illuminate and order all temporal things with which they are closely associated that these may always be effected and grow according to Christ and may be to the glory of the Creator and Redeemer" [LG 31 §2]. The initiative of lay Christians is necessary especially when the matter involves discovering or inventing the means for permeating social, political, and economic realities with the demands of Christian doctrine and life. (CCC 898–899)

Other Particular Vocations

Not all particular or secondary vocations have to do with work. You also have another vocation that is determined by your sex. The Church often talks about the "masculine" and "feminine" vocations and the vocations of motherhood and fatherhood (both spiritual and physical). These vocations are particular missions God has for us as men and women. That is, they are ways that he wants us to reveal his love and nature in the world as men and as women.

In a similar way, parenthood is a vocation. It is a call from God, written into our bodies, to cooperate with him not only in bringing new life into the world, but in forming, educating, and sanctifying those lives so that they too might know and serve God. As the Catechism explains, "In a very special way, parents share in the office of sanctifying 'by leading a conjugal life in the Christian spirit and by seeing to the Christian education of their children' [CIC, can. 835 §4]" (CCC 902).

Then there are some people who are called to identify in a particular way with the sufferings of Jesus during their lifetime. Some of the saints who have endured great trials on their journey to heaven are often spoken about as having a "vocation" to suffering.

There also are vocations to embrace a particular spirituality or a particular form of service in the Church. Some people feel called to live their Catholic Faith as part of lay ecclesial movements such as Communion and Liberation, Opus Dei, or Focolare. These lay movements can help structure a person's prayer life or spiritual practices. The same can be said for many Third Orders within the Church—lay people who feel called to the charism of a religious order, such as the Dominicans or Franciscans, can become secular members of these orders. They make vows to certain schedules of prayers, habits of service, and other spiritual practices in line with the order's charism while at the same time continuing to live their life in the world.

In terms of service, someone might feel like the Lord is calling them to serve the liturgical or formational work of the Church as a layperson, perhaps as a lector, extraordinary minister of Holy Communion, or volunteer catechist (CCC 903). Others might have a vocation to serve God as a missionary—helping evangelize, educate, or care for people both in the US and in other countries.

All these types of vocations are particular vocations. They are individual calls God issues to us at different times in our lives. They are things God asks us to do as we journey on the path of discipleship to our ultimate vocation: holiness. We don't make solemn vows to undertake these calls, and as the circumstances of our life change, we might leave behind one particular vocation and embrace another. Nevertheless, when we say yes to these calls, when we serve God faithfully and strive to love our neighbor through them, they move us further along the path to holiness. They help us to love more fully, give more generously, work more diligently, and judge more compassionately.

Through studies and work, parenthood and prayer, service and living the truth of our sexuality, we grow in virtue, learning to be kinder, more merciful, more sacrificial, and more honest. In a myriad of ways, these vocations teach us to die to ourselves and our will so that God's will can be done.

The Vocations to a Permanent State in Life

If the universal vocation—holiness—is the path to which God calls us, and if the many and varied particular vocations are the things God calls us to do as we journey along that path, then this final type of vocation— sometimes called the spousal vocation, the primary vocation, or vocations to a permanent state of life—is about who we make that journey (or part of that journey) with.

Over the rest of the book, we'll talk in greater detail about each of these permanent states of life. Here, though, we're just going to briefly introduce them so we can see what they have in common.

The first and most common permanent state of life is marriage. In marriage, one man and one woman give themselves to each other, vowing to love, serve, and honor the other for as long as they both shall live and to welcome children from God so that they can raise those children to know and love God too. On the vocation of marriage, the Catechism states:

> "The intimate community of life and love which constitutes the married state has been established by the Creator and endowed by him with its own proper laws. . . . God himself is the author of marriage" [GS 48 §1]. The vocation to marriage is written in the very nature of man and woman as they came from the hand of the Creator. Marriage is not a purely human institution despite the many variations it may have undergone through the

centuries in different cultures, social structures, and spiritual attitudes. (CCC 1603)

The second permanent state of life is the ministerial priesthood or Holy Orders. Traditionally, Holy Orders have been conferred in three degrees: bishops, presbyters (priests), and deacons (CCC 1593). In the Sacrament of Holy Orders, a man receives a special grace of the Holy Spirit, which "configures" him to Christ "so that he may serve . . . as a representative of Christ, Head of the Church, in his triple office of priest, prophet, and king" (CCC 1581).

While in marriage the man and woman take each other as spouse, the ordained minister, in a sense, takes the Church, which is the Bride of Christ, as his spouse. His life becomes one of love and service for the Bride. Likewise, similar to the Sacrament of Holy Matrimony where no one has a right to marry, no one has a right to be ordained. Rather, the man must be called by God to enter such a vocation and the Church must confirm that call. The Catechism explains:

> No one has a *right* to receive the sacrament of Holy Orders. Indeed no one claims this office for himself; he is called to it by God [cf. Heb 5:4]. Anyone who thinks he recognizes the signs of God's call to the ordained ministry must humbly submit his desire to the authority of the Church, who has the responsibility and right to call someone to receive orders. Like every grace this sacrament can be *received* only as an unmerited gift. (CCC 1578)

The third permanent state in life is consecrated life. Both men and women can live this vocation, and they can live it in two primary ways: in community or in solitude (CCC 917). Typically, those who live this vocation in community do so with a religious order as a religious brother or sister (such as a Franciscan or Benedictine) or a member of a society of apostolic life. Those who undertake consecrated life in solitude typically live either as a consecrated virgin, widow, or anchoress (women); as a hermit (men); or as a consecrated member of a secular institute (both men and women).

All those who live this vocation are called to it by God. They also typically make three vows: poverty, chastity, and obedience. Through the radical living out of those vows—called "the evangelical counsels"—consecrated men and women seek a closer, more intimate union with Christ. In effect, they give themselves to him in an exclusive and abiding way. They take Christ as their spouse, seeking to live now, on earth, the relationship we all hope to live in eternity. These consecrated men and women are a sign for us of the life to come. Or, as the Catechism states, they "propose . . . to give themselves to God who is loved above all and, pursuing the perfection of charity in the service of the Kingdom, to signify and proclaim in the Church the glory of the world to come [cf. CIC, can. 573]" (CCC 916).

Enduring, Committed, and Called

Marriage, the ministerial priesthood, and consecrated life are all considered permanent states of life in that they are enduring. A valid, sacramental marriage can end only with the death of one of the spouses. The priest (or deacon, or bishop) can be removed from his ministry at the order of a Church tribunal, but the effects of the sacrament on his soul remain. The consecrated man or woman can be freed from their vows but, again, only by their religious superior or bishop.

These states of life are also committed or vowed states of life—when one marries, is ordained, or enters consecrated life, one makes solemn promises either to another person or to God.

Lastly, each of these vocations requires a call. In Holy Matrimony, not only must the one person ask the other to marry them but the Church must, in a sense, confirm that call by discerning if both people are free to marry in the Church. Not everyone can marry; those who are already married or only civilly divorced, those who are not mentally or physically able to give themselves in marriage, and those who wish to marry a member of the same sex are not able to receive the Sacrament of Holy Matrimony. Similarly, God must call someone to Holy Orders or consecrated life, and then that call must be confirmed, either by the Church (in the case of Holy Orders), by a religious order or society (in the case of those wishing to live the consecrated life in community), or by the bishop or secular institute (for those wishing to live the consecrated life in solitude).

In sum, if the universal vocation of holiness is the path to which God calls us and our particular vocations are what we do on that path, then our vocation to a permanent state in life is with whom we walk the path: our husband or wife, the Church, or Christ himself.

The Single State in Life

But what about those who remain single all their lives? Who never marry, receive Holy Orders, or enter consecrated life? Is that a vocation?

The Church hasn't addressed this question head-on, but no magisterial documents refer to a "single" vocation. And, just at face value, the single life is very different from marriage, Holy Orders, or consecrated life, which are enduring vocations. With those vocations, once you give yourself to another—God, the Church, a husband or wife—you can't give yourself to anyone else, a least not without the intervention of death, a tribunal, or your superior. That can't be said of unconsecrated singles. They remain free, at least in theory, to make a permanent gift of themselves to another at any point.

Likewise, marriage, Holy Orders, and consecrated life require solemn vows before God and man. Unconsecrated singles don't take any vows. Finally, calls to the vocations of marriage, Holy Orders, and consecrated life are all confirmed by the Church in some way. This is not the case for people who are single—only when they choose to leave the single life and enter one of the three permanent states in life is there any confirmation of calling.

Likely for this reason, the Church doesn't talk about the single life as a vocation but rather as a temporary state in life. This might be your state in life right now. But eventually, you will most likely leave this state in life and enter a new one. You will get married, become a priest, or enter consecrated life. For those who remain single throughout their life (or even just longer than they would like), the Catechism has this to say:

We must also remember the great number of *single persons* who, because of the particular circumstances in which they have to live—often not of their choosing—are especially close to Jesus' heart and therefore deserve the special affection and active solicitude of the Church, especially of pastors. Many remain *without a human family,* often due to conditions of poverty. Some live their situation in the spirit of the Beatitudes, serving God and neighbor in exemplary fashion. The doors of homes, the "domestic churches," and of the great family which is the Church must be open to all of them. "No one is without a family in this world: the Church is a home and family for everyone, especially those who 'labor and are heavy laden'" [FC 85; cf. Mt 11:28]. (CCC 1658)

In other words, because of illness, accident, confused reason, or sin (their own or another's), not everyone enters the vocation to which they're called (or enters it at a typical age). This can be a tremendous cross for many people, and we're called to reach out to and care for single people, especially older people, in a special way. In turn, those who find themselves unable to enter the vocation to which they believe God has called them, either temporarily or indefinitely, are to look for ways they can serve him now, in their single state. For, "like all the lay faithful," they are:

> entrusted by God with the apostolate by virtue of their Baptism and Confirmation, they have the right and duty, individually or grouped in associations, to work so that the divine message of salvation may be known and accepted by all men throughout the earth. This duty is the more pressing when it is only through them that men can hear the Gospel and know Christ. Their activity in ecclesial communities is so necessary that, for the most part, the apostolate of the pastors cannot be fully effective without it [cf. LG 33]. (CCC 900)

SELECTED READING
Second Vatican Council, Dogmatic Constitution on the Church *Lumen Gentium* (November 21, 1964), no. 41

The classes and duties of life are many, but holiness is one—that sanctity which is cultivated by all who are moved by the Spirit of God, and who obey the voice of the Father and worship God the Father in spirit and in truth. These people follow the poor Christ, the humble and cross-bearing Christ in order to be worthy of being sharers in His glory. Every person must walk unhesitatingly according to his own personal gifts and duties in the path of living faith, which arouses hope and works through charity.

In the first place, the shepherds of Christ's flock must holily and eagerly, humbly and courageously carry out their ministry, in imitation of the eternal high Priest, the Shepherd and Guardian of our souls. They ought to fulfill this duty in such a way that it will be the principal means also of their own sanctification. Those chosen for the fullness of the priesthood are granted the ability of exercising the perfect duty of pastoral charity by the grace of the sacrament of Orders. This perfect duty of pastoral charity is exercised in every form of episcopal care and service, prayer, sacrifice and preaching. By this same sacramental grace, they are given the courage necessary to lay down their lives for their sheep, and the ability of promoting greater holiness in the Church by their daily example, having become a pattern for their flock.

Priests, who resemble bishops to a certain degree in their participation of the sacrament of Orders, form the spiritual crown of the bishops. They participate in the grace of their office and they should grow daily in their love of God and their neighbor by the exercise of their office through Christ, the eternal and unique Mediator. They should preserve the bond of priestly communion, and they should abound in every spiritual good and thus present to all men a living witness to God. All this they should do in emulation of those priests who often, down through the course of the centuries, left an outstanding example of the holiness of humble and hidden service. Their praise lives on in the Church of God. By their very office of praying and offering sacrifice for their own people and the entire people of God, they should rise to greater holiness. Keeping in mind what they are doing and imitating what they are handling, these priests, in their apostolic labors, rather than being ensnared by perils and hardships, should rather rise to greater holiness through these perils and hardships. They should ever nourish and strengthen their action from an abundance of contemplation, doing all this for the comfort of the entire Church of God. All priests, and especially those who are called "diocesan priests," due to the special title of their ordination, should keep continually before their minds the fact that their faithful loyalty toward and their generous cooperation with their bishop is of the greatest value in their growth in holiness.

Ministers of lesser rank are also sharers in the mission and grace of the Supreme Priest. In the first place among these ministers are deacons, who, in as much as they are dispensers of Christ's mysteries and servants of the Church, should keep themselves free from every vice and stand before men as personifications of goodness and friends of God. Clerics, who are called by the Lord and are set aside as His portion in order to prepare themselves for the various ministerial offices under the watchful eye of spiritual shepherds, are bound to bring their hearts and minds into accord with this special election (which is theirs). They will accomplish this by their constancy in prayer, by their burning love, and by their unremitting recollection of whatever is true, just and of good repute. They will accomplish all this for the glory and honor of God. Besides these already named, there are also laymen, chosen of God and called by the bishop. These laymen spend themselves completely in apostolic labors, working the Lord's field with much success.

Furthermore, married couples and Christian parents should follow their own proper path (to holiness) by faithful love. They should sustain one another in grace throughout the entire length of their lives. They should embue their offspring, lovingly welcomed as God's gift, with Christian doctrine and the evangelical virtues. In this manner, they offer all men the example of unwearying and generous love; in this way they build up the brotherhood of charity; in so doing, they stand as the witnesses and cooperators in the fruitfulness of Holy Mother Church; by such lives, they are a sign and a participation in that very love, with which Christ loved His Bride and for which He delivered Himself up for her. A like example, but one given in a different way, is that offered by widows and single people, who are able to make great contributions toward holiness and apostolic endeavor in the Church. Finally, those who engage in labor—and frequently it is of a heavy nature—should better themselves by their human labors. They should be of aid to their fellow citizens. They should raise all of society, and even creation itself, to a better mode of existence. Indeed, they should imitate by their lively charity, in their joyous hope and by their voluntary sharing of each others' burdens, the very Christ who plied His hands with carpenter's tools and Who in union with His Father, is continually working for the salvation of all men. In this, then, their daily work they should climb to the heights of holiness and apostolic activity.

May all those who are weighed down with poverty, infirmity and sickness, as well as those who must bear various hardships or who suffer persecution for justice sake—may they all know they are united with the suffering Christ in a special way for the salvation of the world. The Lord called them blessed in His Gospel and they are those whom "the God of all graces, who has called us unto His eternal glory in Christ Jesus, will Himself, after we have suffered a little while, perfect, strengthen and establish."

Finally all Christ's faithful, whatever be the conditions, duties and circumstances of their lives—and indeed through all these, will daily increase in holiness, if they receive all things with faith from the hand of their Heavenly Father and if they cooperate with the divine will. In this temporal service, they will manifest to all men the love with which God loved the world.

QUESTIONS FOR REVIEW

1. Define "particular vocations." Give three examples.
2. How can a job be a vocation?
3. What does it mean to have a vocation to suffering?
4. What are the three permanent states in life?
5. What do all three permanent states in life have in common?

QUESTIONS FOR DISCUSSION

1. When you think about your future career, do you think about it more in terms of the money it will earn you or the service you can render through it? Why? Do the Church's teachings on vocations challenge you to think about a career differently?
2. Who is a couple you know living the vocation of marriage or a person you know living the vocation to Holy Orders or consecrated life who inspires you through their vocation? What about the way they live makes that vocation attractive to you?
3. To what permanent state in life do you think God might be calling you?

Chapter 3

"Serve One Another"

In the kingdom of God, every vocation is important. Every vocation is, in fact, essential. And no vocation is lived in isolation from the other vocations.

Sign and Help

First, each vocation is a sign to the others. For example, those living the consecrated vocation help the whole Church better understand "the mystery of redemption" (CCC 932). Pope St. John Paul II tells us that this vocation also "manifests the inner nature of the Christian calling and the striving of the whole Church as Bride towards union with her one Spouse."[1]

Similarly, those living the vocation of marriage are a sign of the relationship between Christ and his Church (Eph 5:31–32), of the "covenant of salvation" (CCC 2384), and of the loving communion within the Trinity. "Man becomes the image of God not so much in the moment of solitude," writes John Paul II in his *Theology of the Body*, "as in the moment of communion."[2]

---

[1] Pope John Paul II, Apostolic Exhortation on the Consecrated Life and its Mission in the Church and in the World *Vita Consecrata* (March 25, 1996), §3.

[2] Pope John Paul II, The Redemption of the Body and Sacramentality of Marriage (Theology of the Body) (September 5, 1979–November 28, 1984), 9:3.

Then there are those living the vocation of Holy Orders. The ordained man, says the Catechism, "is the sign and the instrument of God's merciful love for the sinner" (CCC 1465). Moreover, quoting Pope Pius XII and St. Thomas Aquinas, the Catechism continues:

> In the ecclesial service of the ordained minister, it is Christ himself who is present to his Church as Head of his Body, Shepherd of his flock, high priest of the redemptive sacrifice, Teacher of Truth. This is what the Church means by saying that the priest, by virtue of the sacrament of Holy Orders, acts *in persona Christi Capitis* [cf. LG 10; 28; SC 33; CD 11; PO 2; 6]:

> "It is the same priest, Christ Jesus, whose sacred person his minister truly represents. Now the minister, by reason of the sacerdotal consecration which he has received, is truly made like to the high priest and possesses the authority to act in the power and place of the person of Christ himself (*virtute ac persona ipsius Christi*)" [Pius XII, encyclical, *Mediator Dei*: AAS, 39 (1947) 548].

> "Christ is the source of all priesthood: the priest of the old law was a figure of Christ, and the priest of the new law acts in the person of Christ" [St. Thomas Aquinas, *STh* III, 22, 4c]. (CCC 1548)

Just as each vocation is a sign to the other vocations, helping us to understand heavenly realities, each vocation is also a help to each one of us. For example, Holy Orders "has been instituted for the good of men and the communion of the Church" (CCC 1551). Through the ministerial priesthood the people of God receive the sacraments, which fill us with sanctifying grace (the life of God), strengthen that life within us, and restore it to us when we lose that grace through sin. Priests are also our representatives before God. Like Moses and Abraham in the Old Testament, they intercede for us and for the whole world, "presenting to God the prayer of the Church" (CCC 1552).

Configured to Christ and joined to their bishops, priests uniquely participate in Christ's mission as priest, prophet, and king, offering the Eucharistic sacrifice, proclaiming the Good News in the assembly, and governing Christ's Church. This mission is exercised most fully by those who possess "the fullness of the Sacrament of Holy Orders," the bishops (CCC 1557). As the Vatican II document *Lumen Gentium* states:

> Episcopal consecration, together with the office of sanctifying, also confers the office of teaching and of governing. . . . For . . . by means of the imposition of hands and the words of consecration, the grace of the Holy Spirit is so conferred, and the sacred character so impressed, that bishops in an eminent and visible way sustain the roles of Christ Himself as Teacher, Shepherd and High Priest, and that they act in His person.[3]

Those who enter the consecrated life are a help to the other vocations in a variety of ways, depending on the form of life followed and the particular charism embraced. Through prayer, teaching, care for the sick and orphaned, the proclamation of the Gospel, or missionary work, consecrated men and women serve the Body of Christ (CCC 931). They also help the rest of the Body better understand how to live the teachings of Christ.

> For those who are on this "narrower" path encourage their brethren by their example, and bear striking witness "that the world cannot be transfigured and offered to God without the spirit of the Beatitudes" [LG 31 §2]. (CCC 932)

Lastly, Christian married couples and their children form the "domestic church," a community of "faith, hope, and charity" with an "evangelizing and missionary task" (CCC 2203–2205). That task is to make Christ present in their homes and in the culture, forming their children in the faith and bringing the Gospel to offices and schools, neighborhoods and

---

[3] Second Vatican Council, Dogmatic Constitution on the Church *Lumen Gentium* (November 21, 1964), §21.

shops. Families go where priests and consecrated individuals rarely do, giving them the responsibility for making Christ present in every corner of society. Single lay people share in this mission.

The Catechism also notes:

> It is not the role of the Pastors of the Church to intervene directly in the political structuring and organization of social life. This task is part of the vocation of the *lay faithful*, acting on their own initiative with their fellow citizens. Social action can assume various concrete forms. It should always have the common good in view and be in conformity with the message of the Gospel and the teaching of the Church. It is the role of the laity "to animate temporal realities with Christian commitment, by which they show that they are witnesses and agents of peace and justice" [SRS 47 §6; cf. 42]. (CCC 2442)

Discerning Your Vocation

God calls each of us to follow and serve him in a unique way. Hearing that call and understanding it is called "discernment." When we discern something, we are making judgments about the truth of something. We are deciding what is right and what is wrong. When we discern our vocations, we are deciding what is the right path for us—the path to which God is calling us. This process of discerning the various vocations to which God calls you—both your particular vocation and your permanent state in life—begins with a recognition that every vocation is a call to serve.

During his lifetime, Jesus Christ called us to love one another as he loved us. He loved us "to the end," suffering and dying for the sake of our eternal salvation (CCC 1823). He called us to care for the poor, the widowed, the orphaned, and the mistreated. He also called us to value people's eternal good (and our own eternal good) above all else, proclaiming the Good News and baptizing the people of all nations in the name of the Father, Son, and Holy Spirit (Matt 28:19).

As such, whether God calls you to teach or to heal, to balance a company's books or run your own small business, to be a priest or a nun, a husband or a wife, he is calling you to serve—to serve the common good, to care for those often overlooked or mistreated by others, and to proclaim the Gospel, both through your example and your words. You are to be the hands and feet of Christ in the world.

On a more practical level, discerning your vocation requires prayerful attentiveness to God's call and the opportunities he puts before you.

Every once in a great while, God speaks to us directly, using extraordinary means—words of knowledge, signs, even apparitions—to make his will clear. We see this in the Book of Acts, when Jesus knocks St. Paul off his horse and tells him to stop persecuting Christians, and when an angel appears to St. Philip in a dream and urges him on to Gaza (Acts 9:3–5; 8:26).

God can and occasionally does still make his will known to us in these ways. But, more often, he speaks to us through our desires, abilities, and opportunities. Above, we talked about how a desire to write, the ability to write, and the opportunity to write are all good signs that God could be calling you to serve him as a writer. In a similar way, the desire to marry, the ability to marry freely in the Church, and the opportunity to marry are all good signs God is calling you to marriage. Or perhaps you have a desire to spend your days in prayer and find yourself easily making time to talk to God throughout the day or spending time in adoration. Those are good signs you should pray about entering a religious order dedicated to contemplative or intercessory prayer. You might also have the desire to serve the Church as a priest, to offer the Mass, preach, and celebrate the sacraments. Those desires paired with ability and opportunity are a sign God might be calling you to the priesthood.

It's not always easy, of course, to discern our desires. Sometimes we feel both a call to marriage and a call to serve God as a priest or religious. Our hearts can feel torn. Or we might feel a strong call to marriage, but no opportunity seems to present itself. This is where prayer and good spiritual guidance are so important.

The more time we spend with God, the more attuned we become to hearing his voice. Also, the more we strive to do his will in the little things, the more our wills become conformed to his in the big things. His desires for us not only become clear but they become our desires for ourselves.

Having a trusted priest or spiritual advisor who knows us and can help us sort through our conflicting emotions or desires is also essential. Then, as we progress through the discernment process, the Church will also be there for us, helping young men discern their call to the priesthood through the seminary application and formation process; working through the bishop or religious superiors as someone moves forward in discerning consecrated life; and helping us prepare for marriage and be certain of our choice to marry a particular person through the marriage preparation process.

This process of discernment is sometimes easy and quick, sometimes long and difficult. But God never calls you to a vocation that isn't right for you and isn't ultimately what you desire. He doesn't drag anyone kicking and screaming into a monastery or convent. He doesn't force anyone to become a priest. He doesn't demand that anyone marry against their will. He gently invites you to the vocation that will fulfill your desires, help you become the person he made you to be, and draw you closer to your ultimate vocation: holiness.

Preparing for Your Vocation

As we look more closely at each of the three permanent states in life, we'll talk more about the formal process of preparation for each vocation. Whether you are preparing to marry, to enter Holy Orders, or to live the consecrated life, the Church has specific steps of preparation she'll ask you to take. Those steps will differ depending on the vocation for which you are preparing to enter. Long before you begin that formal preparation, however, there are certain steps you need to take that will help you prepare equally for all three vocations.

The first step is simply growing closer to God. God loves you, wants the best for you, and wills the best for you. But you have to know God in order to know that. The more you learn about God and his love, the more you come to understand how he has worked throughout Salvation History to draw the whole world closer to himself, the more you will come to love him and trust him with your life. So read about him in the Scriptures. Study him even outside of religion class. Receive him in the Eucharist. And spend time with him in prayer.

Developing a healthy prayer life is so essential to preparing for a vocation that it's really its own step. If you never talk with someone, you can never really get to know them. And if you never listen to someone, you can never really hear or understand what they have to say. The more you talk to God and listen to him (which is all prayer really is), the more you'll come to understand not just what his will for your life is but also the ways you need to grow and heal so that you can pursue his will.

Each of us carries wounds in our heart. Some of those wounds are there because of things we've done to ourselves—wrongs we've done or good actions we've failed to do. Other wounds are there because of what others have done to us. Sometimes the very people who are supposed to love, protect, and support us let us down. Sometimes they hurt us in grievous and deeply sinful ways. Unless we take those wounds to God, a trusted spiritual advisor, and sometimes a trusted counselor, those wounds can linger in our souls, holding us back from living the lives God wants us to live. Seeking healing from our wounds is an important step in preparing for our vocation. The more healing we find, the more free we will be to follow God wherever and whenever he calls.

The pursuit of virtue is yet another critical part of the preparation process. Every day you are faced with hundreds of different choices that will help you either grow in virtue or vice. You can choose to speak ill of a person or speak well of them; you can choose to hold on to a grudge or extend forgiveness; you can choose to be lazy or work hard; you can choose to offer to help out around the house or you can hide in your bedroom and play games on your phone.

All these choices can seem like little things in the moment, but each choice is shaping your character, making you into the person you will be for all eternity. Good choices make you, day by day, into a just person, a kind person, a selfless person, a generous person. Bad choices make you, day by day, into an unjust person, a cruel person, a selfish person, and a greedy person. Ask yourself: who do you want to be? Then make the choices that help you become that person. Seeking to grow in virtue makes it easier for you to hear God and follow God. It will be easier for you to live your vocation in such a way that other people are helped and attracted to God. And, ultimately, it will help you choose God at the end of your days.

One of the most important virtues you can develop right now is the virtue of chastity. The Church doesn't teach that sex is a bad thing. The Church teaches that sex is a holy thing, ordained by God to bring husbands and wives closer together and to bring new life into the world. We'll talk more about that in Part II. For now, what's important to know is that sexual sin, like all sin, wounds us. It hurts us in ways that make it harder for us to understand our own dignity and others' dignity. It also makes it harder for us to hear God's voice and love others as he asks us to love them.

Sexual sin before marriage can affect our ability to discern a vocation and live that vocation. This is true of all forms of sexual sin: pornography, masturbation, "sexting," acting on same-sex attractions, and sexual acts with another person outside of marriage. Saying no to sexual sin and yes to healthy, chaste friendships with your peers is integral to your ability to give yourself to another, to the Church, or to God himself later in life.

With grace, healing is always possible if you've sinned. God is always waiting and wanting to forgive us. There is nothing you can do that he will not forgive if you ask him to in the Sacrament of Confession. But while forgiveness can happen in an instant, healing usually takes time. It can take many years, either interfering with your ability to enter into a vocation or interfering with your ability to joyfully live that vocation.

The last thing you can do to ready your heart for God's call is to receive the sacraments. The more you go to Confession and the more you receive the Eucharist, the more God's life is strengthened in you. There is real grace in those sacraments. There is also real grace in simply sitting in Christ's presence in Eucharistic Adoration. That grace will draw you closer to God. It will help you to make good choices and grow in virtue. It will help you to heal from all the wounds in your heart, freeing you to love. And it will help you practice chastity, saving your body and your heart for the vocation God has for you.

SELECTED READING
Pope Francis, Post-Synodal Apostolic Exhortation to Young
People and to the Entire People of God *Christus Vivit*
(March 25, 2019), nos. 250–257

The first thing we need to discern and discover is this: Jesus wants to
be a friend to every young person. This discernment is the basis of
all else. In the risen Lord's dialogue with Simon Peter, his great question was: "Simon, son of John, do you love me?" (Jn 21:16). In other
words, do you love me as a friend? The mission that Peter received
to shepherd Jesus' flock will always be linked to this gratuitous love,
this love of friendship.

On the other hand, there was the unsuccessful encounter of
Jesus and the rich young man, which clearly shows that the young
man failed to perceive the Lord's loving gaze (cf. Mk 10:21). He
went away sorrowful, despite his original good intentions, because
he could not turn his back on his many possessions (cf. Mt 19:22).
He missed the opportunity of what surely would have been a great
friendship. We will never know what that one young man, upon
whom Jesus gazed with love and to whom he stretched out his hand,
might have been for us, what he might have done for mankind.

"The life that Jesus gives us is a love story, a *life history* that wants
to blend with ours and sink roots in the soil of our own lives. That
life is not salvation up 'in the cloud' and waiting to be downloaded,
a new 'app' to be discovered, or a technique of mental self-improve-
ment. Still less is that life a 'tutorial' for finding out the latest news.
The salvation that God offers us is *an invitation to be part of a love
story* interwoven with our personal stories; it is alive and wants to be
born in our midst so that we can bear fruit just as we are, wherever we
are and with everyone all around us. The Lord comes there to sow
and to be sown."

I would now like to speak of vocation in the strict sense, as a call
to missionary service to others. The Lord calls us to share in his work
of creation and to contribute to the common good by using the gifts
we have received.

This missionary vocation thus has to do with service. For our life on earth reaches full stature when it becomes an offering. Here I would repeat that "the mission of being in the heart of the people is not just a part of my life or a badge I can take off; it is not an 'extra' or just another moment in life. Instead, it is something I cannot uproot from my being without destroying my very self. I am a mission on this earth; that is the reason why I am here in this world." It follows that every form of pastoral activity, formation and spirituality should be seen in the light of our Christian vocation.

Your own personal vocation does not consist only in the work you do, though that is an expression of it. Your vocation is something more: it is a path guiding your many efforts and actions towards service to others. So in discerning your vocation, it is important to determine if you see in yourself the abilities needed to perform that specific service to society.

This gives greater value to everything you do. Your work stops being just about making money, keeping busy or pleasing others. It becomes your vocation because you are called to it; it is something more than merely a pragmatic decision. In the end, it is a recognition of why I was made, why I am here on earth, and what the Lord's plan is for my life. He will not show me every place, time, and detail since I will have to make my own prudent decisions about these. But he will show me a direction in life, for he is my Creator and I need to listen to his voice, so that, like clay in the hands of a potter, I can let myself be shaped and guided by him. Then I will become what I was meant to be, faithful to my own reality.

To respond to our vocation, we need to foster and develop all that we are. This has nothing to do with inventing ourselves or creating ourselves out of nothing. It has to do with finding our true selves in the light of God and letting our lives flourish and bear fruit. "In God's plan, every man and woman is meant to seek self-fulfilment, for every human life is called to some task by God." Your vocation inspires you to bring out the best in yourself for the glory of God and the good of others. It is not simply a matter of doing things, but of doing them with meaning and direction. Saint Alberto Hurtado told young people to think very seriously about the direction their lives should take: "If the helmsman of a ship becomes careless, he is fired straightaway for not taking his sacred responsibility seriously. As for our lives, are we fully aware of the course they are taking? What course is your life taking? If it is necessary to give this more thought, I would beg each one of you to give it the highest consideration, because to get it right is tantamount to success; to err is quite simply to fail."

QUESTIONS FOR REVIEW

1. Give an example of how one permanent state in life can serve another state in life.
2. What is an extraordinary way God communicates his will for our life to us?
3. What are the ordinary ways God communicates his will to us?
4. What are two things you can do right now, besides prayer, to prepare for whatever God is calling you to?
5. Why is prayer such an important part of discerning a vocation and preparing for it?

QUESTIONS FOR DISCUSSION

1. Has God ever communicated his will in an extraordinary way to you? If so, describe. Why do you think God doesn't usually communicate with us in this way?
2. What are some of the choices you've already faced today to grow in virtue or vice? How did you respond? Why?
3. Can you think of some ways that sexual sin might make it difficult to follow God and live your vocation? Explain.

Part II

Holy Matrimony

In many ways, the story of Salvation History—the story of God's plan to make us saints—is a love story. It's the story of God creating us out of love, losing us to sin, and then pursuing us through time in order to win us back. This is one of the reasons why the Bible is shot through with marital imagery.

Think about it for a minute. The Bible begins with a marriage: the marriage of Adam and Eve. It also ends with a marriage: the wedding feast of the Lamb. In between those bookends, the countless references to marriage include the prophets describing God as a husband wedded to a faithless wife (Israel), Jesus performing his first miracle at a wedding, and St. Paul comparing the relationship of husband and wife to the relationship of Christ and his Church.

None of this is a coincidence. Although people in our culture have grown used to thinking of marriage as a human institution, designed by men and reshaped by the laws of men, that's not what marriage is. Or, at least, that's not what marriage is supposed to be. Rather, marriage was designed by God at the creation of the world to be both a natural and supernatural help to men and women. It teaches us about ourselves—how we are to live and love in this world. And it teaches us about God—who he is and how he loves. This is why marriage is a vocation, a holy calling that not only helps us grow in holiness but also equips us to help others grow in holiness.

In order to understand how this is possible, we need to do as Jesus recommended in Matthew 19 and go back to "the beginning."

Chapter 1

Marriage in the Divine Plan

In the Beginning

|| ASSIGNED READING
|| Genesis 2

The Book of Genesis gives us two accounts of the creation of the world. The first account shows God creating the heavens, earth, and everything in them. It is, in a sense, like the panoramic shots we so often see at the beginning of a movie. It gives us the view from thirty thousand feet, helping us to see the "big picture" of creation: that God created the world and that it is "good" (Gen 1:31). The second creation account, in Genesis 2, is more like a close-up. It zeroes in on the creation of man and woman, giving us more details about who our first parents were and how they came to be.

In Genesis 1:27–28, we're simply told:

> So God created man in his own image, in the image of God he created him; male and female he created them. And God blessed them, and God said to them, "Be fruitful and multiply, and fill the earth and subdue it; and have dominion over the fish of the sea and over the birds of the air and over every living thing that moves upon the earth."

In Genesis 2 we learn that God created Adam first: "then the LORD God formed man of dust from the ground, and breathed into his nostrils the breath of life; and man became a living soul" (v. 7). He then put Adam into the Garden of Eden and instructed him to "till it and keep it" (Gen 2:15).

Original Solitude

During his papacy, Pope St. John Paul II gave the Church an important series of reflections on the dignity of the human person, the meaning of the body, and the nature of married love. Collectively, we call these reflections the "Theology of the Body." In the *Theology of the Body*, John Paul II talks about this point in the creation story, when it was just Adam, alone in the Garden with other creatures not like himself. He calls this time "original solitude."[1]

Alone, before God, Adam sees that he is not like the animals that surround him. Only he possesses a rational soul. Only he is made in the image of God. This "original solitude" is an affirmation of the human person's great dignity. At the same time, it also makes Adam suspect that something—or, more specifically, someone—is missing.

And someone is missing. Up to this point, God had affirmed the goodness of everything in creation, with Genesis 1 telling us "And God saw that it was good" at the end of each day of creation. But in Genesis 2:18 we hear that something is not good: "Then the LORD God said, 'It is not good that the man should be alone.'"

In other words, the human person wasn't created to exist in solitude. We were created for communion. We were created for love. We were created for family. After all, we are made in the image of God, and God isn't one Person; he's Three Persons. He is the reality that every true human community, every true human family reflects. "God in his deepest mystery is not a solitude, but a family because he has within himself

---

[1] Pope John Paul II, The Redemption of the Body and Sacramentality of Marriage (Theology of the Body) (September 5, 1979–November 28, 1984), 5:1 (hereafter cited as TOB).

Fatherhood, Sonship, and the essence of the Family, which is Love."[2]

Original Unity

To help man live the life for which he was created, God creates another person. That person isn't just a friend for Adam, though. It's not another man. It's not another Adam. It's Eve, a woman, a wife, one like him, but also one different from him. This woman, Genesis 2 tells us, was created from Adam's side, which signals her equality with man.[3] Like him, she is made in the image of God. She possesses reason, free will, and the ability to give herself away in love. But despite all that, she is still unlike him. Her body is different, and because the Church teaches that the body is the sign of the person and that it expresses the person, it also means that *she* is different—not less than, but also not the same.

Masculinity and femininity, John Paul II tells us, are two reciprocally completing ways of "being a body" and at the same time of being human.[4] So the differences in our bodies aren't just physical. They are ontological—that is, they have to do with our very being. Men and women share the same human nature, but we possess that nature differently. As men and women, we image unique truths about God and we have unique missions in the world. These differences aren't bad. They're good. They make the world a richer, fuller, better place. The world needs male and female, masculine and feminine. Likewise, these differences aren't intended to divide us; they are intended to unite us. As John Paul II writes:

> Femininity finds itself, in a sense, in the presence of masculinity, while masculinity is confirmed through femininity.... The presence of the feminine element, alongside the male element and together with it, signifies an enrichment for man in the whole perspective of his history, including the history of salvation.[5]

---

[2] John Paul II, *Puebla: A Pilgrimage of Faith*, compiled by the Daughters of St. Paul (Boston: St. Paul Editions, 1979), 86.

[3] TOB 8:4.

[4] TOB 10:1.

[5] TOB 10:1.

The Spousal Meaning of the Body

The complementarity of man and woman points to what John Paul II calls "the spousal meaning of the body."[6] Adam, remember, longed for another. He knew he was made to exist "with someone," or, more specifically, "for someone."[7] God confirms this by making Eve. Adam is not disappointed:

> Then the man said,
> "This at last is bone of my bones
> and flesh of my flesh;
> she shall be called Woman,
> because she was taken out of Man."
> Therefore a man leaves his father and his mother and cleaves to
>   his wife, and they become one flesh.
> And the man and his wife were both naked, and were not
>   ashamed. (Gen 2:23–25)

Man and woman complement each other. We complement each other spiritually, with man and woman each bringing something to the other that the other needs. And we complement each other physically. The man's body is made for the woman's body. The woman's body is made for the man's body. Each body makes more sense in light of the other. They "fit" together like puzzle pieces. And when those bodies come together, in the right way and right time, new life comes into being. A third person is born. That doesn't happen with two male bodies. That doesn't happen with two female bodies. Only the man and woman together can image the life-giving love of the Holy Trinity, where the Father pours out his love eternally and completely to the Son; the Son receives that love and pours it right back, eternally and completely; and the love between them is so real, so complete, that it too is a person, the Holy Spirit.

That's what married love is. When a man and woman give themselves

---

6   TOB 102:5.

7   TOB 14:2.

totally, exclusively, and permanently to one another, holding nothing of themselves back—including their fertility—their communion becomes an echo of the life-giving communion within the Holy Trinity. For this reason, John Paul II could write, "Man becomes the image of God not so much in the moment of solitude, but in the moment of communion."[8]

The marital act, of course, isn't the only moment of communion in which man images God. We're made for spiritual communion, not just with our spouse but with friends, family members, and all our brothers and sisters in Christ. We're all made to be a gift to one another and to give ourselves away in love to one another. But married love signifies in full what other types of communion can only signify in part. It is an embodied sign of what the human person is called to do—give oneself away in life-giving love—and of who the Holy Trinity is—an eternal communion of life-giving Love.

Original Innocence

Remember, at first, in the Garden, Adam and Eve were "naked, and were not ashamed." That is, they were living God's plan for man and woman, in marriage, as God intended them to live it. (In the *Theology of the Body*, John Paul II calls the state of their relationship "original unity.") During this time, both were filled with God's life. Each possessed in full what the Church calls the preternatural gifts of bodily immortality, integrity, and infused knowledge. That is, their bodies were capable of living forever, their reason perfectly governed their emotions, and they knew the deepest truths about God, the world, and themselves without ever needing to be taught those truths. Also, they were free of sin; they lived each moment in complete obedience to God. Sin was not part of their world. There was no brokenness, no sadness, no hurt, no woundedness. That's why the *Theology of the Body* calls this point in Salvation History "original innocence."

This moment in the Garden is so important because it shows us how God intended marriage to be from the beginning. It was a loving, inti-

---

[8] TOB 9:3.

mate, exclusive, and permanent relationship between one man and one woman, ordered to mutual help and the creation of new life. It taught man and woman who they were: gifts made for communion with each other. It also taught man and woman something about who God was: that he was faithful, that he was a Communion of Persons, and that his love was life-giving. It helped them understand how God loved them and how God loved in eternity.

Reflecting on what we see in the Garden, at the beginning of human history, the Catechism says:

> God who created man out of love also calls him to love—the fundamental and innate vocation of every human being. For man is created in the image and likeness of God who is himself love [cf. Gen 1:27; 1 Jn 4:8; 16]. Since God created him man and woman, their mutual love becomes an image of the absolute and unfailing love with which God loves man. It is good, very good, in the Creator's eyes. And this love which God blesses is intended to be fruitful and to be realized in the common work of watching over creation: "And God blessed them, and God said to them: 'Be fruitful and multiply, and fill the earth and subdue it'" [Gen 1:28; cf. 1:31]. (CCC 1604)

Unfortunately, this time of original innocence and original unity did not last.

Original Sin

In Genesis 3, the harmony of Eden comes to an end. Eve listens to the serpent, who comes into the Garden to tempt her into sin. Adam, in turn, listens to Eve, and the world is turned upside down. Both Adam and Eve die spiritually that day; they lose the life of God within their souls and, along with it, the preternatural gifts. Their bodies become subject to illness and decay. Their reason no longer perfectly governs their emotions; rather, their passions and desires overrule their reason. And that same reason becomes clouded by sin so that truths they once knew perfectly become less clear to them. It becomes harder for them to know the good and do the good.

With Adam and Eve's sin, disorder comes into the world. The original harmony of creation between humans and animals, humans and nature, and, especially, humans and other humans ends. Animals are no longer subject to man, growing food becomes difficult, and God's plan for human friendship and human marriage goes awry. Some of this is a consequence of sin. Some is a punishment for sin. As God tells Adam and Eve after they confess what they have done:

> To the woman he said,
> "I will greatly multiply your pain in childbearing;
> in pain you shall bring forth children,
> yet your desire shall be for your husband,
> and he shall rule over you."
> And to Adam he said,
> "Because you have listened to the voice of your wife,
> and have eaten of the tree
> of which I commanded you,
> 'You shall not eat of it,'
> cursed is the ground because of you;
> in toil you shall eat of it all the days of your life;
> thorns and thistles it shall bring forth to you;
> and you shall eat the plants of the field.
> In the sweat of your face
> you shall eat bread
> till you return to the ground,
> for out of it you were taken;
> you are dust,
> and to dust you shall return." (Gen 3:16–19)

Adam and Eve's terrible choice brought death and destruction into the world. It also brought death and destruction into the human soul. All their descendants would inherit their human nature, a human nature deprived of the sanctifying grace (God's life) that it was meant to have.

All their descendants would also inherit a tendency to sin (known as "concupiscence"). It would be hard for every single human being to know the good and do the good. This is true in all of life, including marriage.

Original sin made living God's design for man and woman difficult. Lust led men and women to pursue sexual intimacy outside of marriage. It made it difficult to be faithful to only one person and to not treat others as objects for our own sexual satisfaction. Other disordered desires affected marriage as well. As selfishness, greed, lust, wrath, envy, sloth, pride, and vanity worked their way into the human soul, polygamy, adultery, fornication, homosexuality, pornography, contraception, abortion, abuse, and divorce worked their way into the relationships of man and woman.

Eventually, even Moses gave up trying to force the Israelites to live marriage as God intended it, and granted permission for men to divorce their wives (Deut 24:1–3). It seemed as if God's plan for man and woman in marriage was doomed to fail.

But then Jesus Christ came.

The Sign Redeemed

‖ ASSIGNED READING
‖ Ephesians 5:21–33

God's plan was never just to leave humanity broken in our sin. At the same time that he announced the consequences of Adam and Eve's sin, he also announced his plan to redeem the world, promising:

> I will put enmity between you and the woman,
> and between your seed and her seed;
> he shall bruise your head,
> and you shall bruise his heel. (Gen 3:15)

The Redeemer who would come would crush the head of the serpent, meaning he would free humanity from the grip of sin. Satan would no longer rule over us. We could choose another lord, *the* Lord, and he would give us the grace to live the lives he intended us to live and have the marriages he intended us to have. The promised Redeemer wouldn't turn back the clock. He wouldn't erase the consequences of sin. We could still choose Satan's ways over God's ways. We would still struggle with temptations to reject God's plan. But, with grace, living God's plan would be possible once more.

The remainder of the Old Testament is the story of God preparing a people to receive that Redeemer: Jesus Christ, the "seed" of the woman who would crush the head of the serpent. When Jesus came, one of his first public acts was to affirm the inherent goodness of marriage and its place in God's plan for the world. He did this by performing his first public miracle at the wedding in Cana. The Catechism explains:

> On the threshold of his public life Jesus performs his first sign—at his mother's request—during a wedding feast [cf. Jn 2:1–11]. The Church attaches great importance to Jesus' presence at the wedding at Cana. She sees in it the confirmation of the goodness of marriage and the proclamation that thenceforth marriage will be an efficacious sign of Christ's presence. (CCC 1613)

Not long afterwards, Jesus also affirmed God's original plan for marriage, telling the Pharisees that Moses' concession, allowing husbands to divorce their wives, was just that: *Moses'* concession. Not God's. Jesus said to them:

> "Have you not read that he who made them from the beginning made them male and female, and said, 'For this reason a man shall leave his father and mother and be joined to his wife, and the two shall become one'? So they are no longer two but one. What therefore God has joined together, let no man put asunder." (Matt 19:4–6)

But Jesus did more than affirm God's original plan for marriage. He elevated it, giving it a newer and higher purpose and calling spouses to a newer and higher standard. In his Letter to the Ephesians, St. Paul talks about that purpose and standard. In the New Covenant, marriage was to be a sign of "Christ and the Church" and the standard was Christ's love for the Church (Eph 5:32).

> Husbands, love your wives, as Christ loved the Church and gave himself up for her, that he might sanctify her, having cleansed her by the washing of water with the word, that he might present the Church to himself in splendor, without spot or wrinkle or any such thing, that she might be holy and without blemish. Even so husbands should love their wives as their own bodies. He who loves his wife loves himself. For no man ever hates his own flesh, but nourishes and cherishes it, as Christ does the Church, because we are members of his body. (Eph 5:25–30)

SELECTED READING
Pope St. John Paul II, Apostolic Exhortation on the Role of the Christian Family in the Modern World *Familiaris Consortio* (November 22, 1981), nos. 12–13

The communion of love between God and people, a fundamental part of the Revelation and faith experience of Israel, finds a meaningful expression in the marriage covenant which is established between a man and a woman.

For this reason, the central word of Revelation, "God loves His people," is likewise proclaimed through the living and concrete word whereby a man and a woman express their conjugal love. Their bond of love becomes the image and the symbol of the covenant which unites God and His people. And the same sin which can harm the conjugal covenant becomes an image of the infidelity of the people to their God: idolatry is prostitution, infidelity is adultery, disobedience to the law is abandonment of the spousal love of the Lord.

But the infidelity of Israel does not destroy the eternal fidelity of the Lord, and therefore the ever faithful love of God is put forward as the model of the faithful love which should exist between spouses.

The communion between God and His people finds its definitive fulfillment in Jesus Christ, the Bridegroom who loves and gives Himself as the Savior of humanity, uniting it to Himself as His body.

He reveals the original truth of marriage, the truth of the "beginning," and, freeing man from his hardness of heart, He makes man capable of realizing this truth in its entirety.

This revelation reaches its definitive fullness in the gift of love which the Word of God makes to humanity in assuming a human nature, and in the sacrifice which Jesus Christ makes of Himself on the Cross for His bride, the Church. In this sacrifice there is entirely revealed that plan which God has imprinted on the humanity of man and woman since their creation; the marriage of baptized persons thus becomes a real symbol of that new and eternal covenant sanctioned in the blood of Christ. The Spirit which the Lord pours forth gives a new heart, and renders man and woman capable of loving one another as Christ has loved us. Conjugal love reaches that fullness to which it is interiorly ordained, conjugal charity, which is the proper and specific way in which the spouses participate in and are called to live the very charity of Christ who gave Himself on the Cross.

In a deservedly famous page, Tertullian has well expressed the greatness of this conjugal life in Christ and its beauty: "How can I ever express the happiness of the marriage that is joined together by the Church strengthened by an offering, sealed by a blessing, announced by angels and ratified by the Father? . . . How wonderful the bond between two believers with a single hope, a single desire, a single observance, a single service! They are both brethren and both fellow-servants; there is no separation between them in spirit or flesh; in fact they are truly two in one flesh and where the flesh is one, one is the spirit."

Receiving and meditating faithfully on the word of God, the Church has solemnly taught and continues to teach that the marriage of the baptized is one of the seven sacraments of the New Covenant.

Indeed, by means of baptism, man and woman are definitively placed within the new and eternal covenant, in the spousal covenant of Christ with the Church. And it is because of this indestructible insertion that the intimate community of conjugal life and love, founded by the Creator, is elevated and assumed into the spousal charity of Christ, sustained and enriched by His redeeming power.

By virtue of the sacramentality of their marriage, spouses are bound to one another in the most profoundly indissoluble manner. Their belonging to each other is the real representation, by means of the sacramental sign, of the very relationship of Christ with the Church.

Spouses are therefore the permanent reminder to the Church of what happened on the Cross; they are for one another and for the children witnesses to the salvation in which the sacrament makes them sharers. Of this salvation event marriage, like every sacrament, is a memorial, actuation and prophecy: "As a memorial, the sacrament gives them the grace and duty of commemorating the great works of God and of bearing witness to them before their children. As actuation, it gives them the grace and duty of putting into practice in the present, towards each other and their children, the demands of a love which forgives and redeems. As prophecy, it gives them the grace and duty of living and bearing witness to the hope of the future encounter with Christ."

Like each of the seven sacraments, so also marriage is a real symbol of the event of salvation, but in its own way. "The spouses participate in it as spouses, together, as a couple, so that the first and immediate effect of marriage (res et sacramentum) is not supernatural grace itself, but the Christian conjugal bond, a typically Christian communion of two persons because it represents the mystery of Christ's incarnation and the mystery of His covenant. The content of participation in Christ's life is also specific: conjugal love involves a totality, in which all the elements of the person enter—appeal of the body and instinct, power of feeling and affectivity, aspiration of the spirit and of will. It aims at a deeply personal unity, the unity that, beyond union in one flesh, leads to forming one heart and soul; it demands indissolubility and faithfulness in definitive mutual giving; and it is open to fertility (cf. Humanae vitae, 9). In a word it is a question of the normal characteristics of all natural conjugal love, but with a new significance which not only purifies and strengthens them, but raises them to the extent of making them the expression of specifically Christian values."

QUESTIONS FOR REVIEW

1. Who is the author of marriage?
2. What lessons do we learn about man from the time of "original solitude"?
3. What was marriage like in the time of "original innocence" and "original unity"?
4. What does marriage, according to God's design, tell us about God? What does it tell us about ourselves?
5. In the New Covenant, what else did the marriage of man and woman come to signify?

QUESTIONS FOR DISCUSSION

1. What is the most beautiful marriage you've ever witnessed? Describe what made it beautiful.
2. When you look at Christ on the Cross, what does that tell you about his love for you? What do you think it looks like to love one's spouse like Christ loves the Church?
3. How does the Church's understanding of marriage differ from the culture's understanding of marriage?

Chapter 2

Marriage in the New Covenant

For two thousand years, the Catholic Church has taught and defended God's design for marriage, believing that every Christian marriage is meant to be a sign of God's love for his people, a sign of who God is, and a sign of the relationship between Christ and his Church. Every marriage, in a sense, is meant to be a sort of catechism, helping the children brought forth by marriage and all the people who witness that marriage grasp some of the deepest and most important truths about God and the human person.

In order for a marriage to do that well, it must have four important characteristics: it must be free; it must involve the full and total gift of self; it must be faithful; and it must be fruitful. Let's talk a little bit more about what each of those words or phrases mean.

Free

In his encyclical on married love and human life, *Humanae Vitae*, Pope St. Paul VI outlines the four requirements of Christian marriage. The first is that it must be a free choice. He writes that married love "is above all fully human, a compound of sense and spirit."

It is not, then, merely a question of natural instinct or emotional drive. It is also, and above all, an act of the free will, whose trust is such that it is meant not only to survive the joys and sorrows of daily life, but also to grow, so that husband and wife become in a way one heart and one soul, and together attain their human fulfillment.[1]

Remember, when God created man and woman, he gave us the power to choose between right and wrong. He made us free: free to love, free to serve, free to obey. We can choose to do those things—or we can choose not to do those things. God doesn't force us into a relationship with him. He always wants us to choose it.

That freedom is one of the ways we image God. God freely *chose* to create the world and to create us. He *chose* to share his life and love with us. And then he *chose* to die on a cross for us. He didn't have to do that. He wasn't obliged to do it. But he wanted to do it, so that's what he chose. He wants the same from us. He wants our love for him and our love for each other to be freely chosen.

That's why human marriages, in the order of grace, must be freely chosen. Of your own free will, you must say, "Yes, I choose to give myself to this person." Marriages in which one or both people are forced to marry or in which their freedom is in some way inhibited (for example, by drug or alcohol addiction) are not considered valid marriages by the Church.

Once you are married, you must, in a sense, keep choosing that person every day. The choice once made is fixed. You can't un-choose your spouse in a valid sacramental marriage. That bond will last "until death do us part." But the bond grows stronger and the marriage grows happier when both spouses consciously choose to love each other every day.

As Paul VI implies above, emotions come and go. Some days you will feel tremendous affection for your spouse. Other days, you might feel irritation or anger or disappointment. But the happiest marriages rise

---

[1] Pope Paul VI, Encyclical Letter on the Regulation of Birth *Humanae Vitae* (July 25, 1968), §9 (hereafter cited as HV).

above those ever-changing emotions because the spouses choose each other—they choose to love each other through their actions—every day. Those choices, over time, make husband and wife "one heart and one soul," enabling them to attain the communion with one another for which we all were made.

Full and Total

God is love. What we possess, he *is*. Because his very nature is love, he loves completely. He holds nothing back. His love is total. This is true in the Holy Trinity, where the Father, Son, and Holy Spirit give completely of themselves to one another (CCC 255). This is also true in the Church, where Christ holds nothing back from his Bride. He gives his life, his Spirit, his sonship to her in total (CCC 766).

Because married love is meant to image this divine love, it too must be total. "It demands a total and definitive gift of persons to one another [cf. FC 80]" (CCC 2391). What does this mean, though, to give yourself to another?

First, it means that you enter into marriage with the full intention of remaining married "until death do us part." There are no "trial" Christian marriages. You don't marry a person with the thought, "If this doesn't work out, there's always divorce." If you give yourself with reservations like that, you're not really giving yourself at all.

Making a full and total gift of yourself also means that you enter into marriage with the full intention of sharing your life together: the good, the bad, the beautiful, the heartbreaking. You commit to being there for your spouse through all the joys and trials of life. You don't reserve the right to leave if the hand you're dealt is more difficult than you anticipated: if one of you gets sick, loses a job, is injured in an accident, struggles with infertility, becomes depressed, or disappoints the other in some other way.

Giving yourself also means that you commit to putting your marriage first—before your career, before your hobbies, before your friends. It doesn't require you to abandon every dream, interest, or personal goal.

A happy, healthy marriage helps both people become more of who they are, not less. But it does require that both spouses care more about their relationship with each other than they care about themselves, and that both spouses, at times, make sacrifices for the good of the family.

Lastly, giving yourself to another means that you share all of who you are with that person. You share your thoughts and your feelings, your memories of the past and your hopes for the future, your plans for the day and your dreams of eternity. In other words, you must be totally and completely yourself with the person you marry. There can be no facades, no masks, no secrets. You must be you, and they must be them.

Faithful

God is faithful to his promises and to his people. In Genesis 3:15, he promised Adam and Eve to send a redeemer to the world; and he did. In Genesis 12, he promised Abraham that he would give him a son in his old age and make a great nation of his descendants; and he did. In Exodus 24, God made a covenant with Israel, promising them that he would be their God and they would be his people; and he honored that covenant. No matter how many times Israel disobeyed, no matter how many false gods they worshipped, no matter how many Jews preferred Babylon to Jerusalem, God remained faithful to his people. Every time Israel strayed or failed or forgot, God remembered and forgave.

In the New Covenant, Jesus does the same for his Church. No matter how many times her members sin, no matter how many times her leaders fail, no matter how many times her priests neglect their duties, Jesus remains faithful to his Bride. His Spirit never abandons the Church. Her sacraments always are efficacious—they always deliver the grace they promise—and his forgiveness is always there for those who ask.

This is the faithfulness Christian marriages are called to imitate. "Married love is . . . faithful and exclusive of all other," writes Paul VI in *Humanae Vitae*. "Though this fidelity of husband and wife sometimes presents difficulties, no one has the right to assert that it is impossible."[2]

In their marriage vows, couples solemnly pledge to be faithful to one another. They swear before God and others that they will give themselves—their body, their love, their affection—to no one else. With those vows, they are rejecting adultery, polygamy, pornography, and divorce, which are all ways of betraying faithful love (CCC 2381–2387).

Divorce and Annulments

There is never, under any circumstances, a reason that can make adultery, polygamy, or the use of pornography okay. They are always and everywhere wrong. Divorce, however, is a bit more nuanced. It is, of course, always a tragedy. It breaks "the contract, to which the spouses freely consented," "does injury to the covenant of salvation, of which sacramental marriage is the sign," and "introduces disorder into the family and into society" (CCC 2384–2385). Civil divorces do not end a sacramental marriage. If a couple is validly married in the eyes of God, no government can change that. And if a person who is civilly divorced, but validly married, enters into a civil marriage with another person, they are committing the sin of adultery.

All who have sinned against marital fidelity—people who have unjustly abandoned their spouse, people who have remarried civilly while they are still married sacramentally to another, people who are in an adulterous relationship, and people who use pornography—are in a state of serious sin. They must not receive Holy Communion (or other sacraments such as Baptism, Confirmation, Holy Matrimony, or Holy Orders), unless they are in danger of death or until they change their situation and confess the sin to a priest. They are not separated from the Church and still have an obligation to attend Mass, but until their sin is repented of and action taken to stop committing the sin, they remain a source of scandal to the community and in a state of mortal sin. Those in illicit civil marriages also are not permitted to serve as godparents or Confirmation sponsors.

---

[2]   HV §9.

At the same time, the Church recognizes that there are valid reasons for the separation of spouses. The Church does not teach that someone must stay in a marriage where there is abuse or where the safety of one spouse or the children is in jeopardy. Those are valid reasons for separation according to the Church's canon law. The Church also tolerates civil divorce after separation, when it is necessary to ensure legal rights, spousal support, and custody agreements (CCC 2383). Likewise, if one of the spouses wishes to petition for an annulment, then a civil divorce is the first step they must take.

An annulment is a recognition by the Church that no valid sacramental marriage ever existed because of some impediment at the time of the wedding ceremony. Annulments don't mean that a civil marriage never existed or that any children born of the union are illegitimate. They simply mean that a valid sacramental marriage never took place. That could be for several reasons, including:

- A defect of consent: one of the spouses did not freely enter into the marriage, either because a person or circumstances forced their hand or because some psychological impediment, such as addiction, prevented them from truly consenting to the act;
- A defect of form: a baptized Catholic was not married before a duly-authorized priest or deacon in the presence of two witnesses;
- Other impediments: for example, a prior marriage of one spouse rendered later attempts at marriages invalid; attempting to marry a close relation (consanguinity); or attempting to marry someone still bound by priestly or religious vows.

One last word on divorce: It's important to always keep in mind that the Church never condemns someone who has been abandoned by their spouse. A person who has been abandoned against their will or a person who has been abandoned and then goes through a civil divorce in order to obtain custody rights or other legal protections has committed no sin. As long as they remain faithful to their marriage vows and do not enter into a romantic relationship with another person, they are still in good standing with the Church and are still free to receive the sacraments. As the Catechism states:

> It can happen that one of the spouses is the innocent victim of a divorce decreed by civil law; this spouse therefore has not contravened the moral law. There is a considerable difference between a spouse who has sincerely tried to be faithful to the sacrament of marriage and is unjustly abandoned, and one who through his own grave fault destroys a canonically valid marriage [cf. FC 84]. (CCC 2386)

Fruitful

You exist because of the love of God. Your friends, your siblings, your parents, and every person who has ever lived has existed because of the love of God. The same holds true for every tree, every flower, every mountain, every drop of water. God holds the whole world in being with his love. His love is why he created the world. Quoting St. Thomas Aquinas, the Catechism says, "God has no other reason for creating than his love and goodness: 'Creatures came into existence when the key of love opened his hand,' [St. Thomas Aquinas, Sent. 2, Prol.]" (CCC 293).

All of creation, in its own way, witnesses to the life-giving nature of God's love. From all eternity, the love of God is fruitful. It isn't sterile. It isn't barren. Rather, it is always generating new life.

Jesus' love for the Church also bears witness to the fruitfulness of God's love. Because of that love, every day, on every continent, men and women are being born anew, through Baptism, as sons and daughters of God.

Human marriages were designed to image this fruitful, life-giving love. Those were God's instructions in the Garden: "Be fruitful and multiply" (Gen 1:28). Those were also God's instructions to Noah and his sons after the flood, to Jacob after he was renamed "Israel," and to all the faithful in the New Covenant (Gen 9:7; 35:11; Jer 23:3). As the Church sees it, it is a tremendous blessing that man and woman, in creating new life, "share in the creative power and fatherhood of God [cf. Eph 3:14; Mt 23:9]" (CCC 2367). The Vatican II document *Gaudium et Spes* adds:

> Parents should regard as their proper mission the task of transmitting human life and educating those to whom it has been transmitted. They should realize that they are thereby cooperators with the love of God the Creator and are, so to speak, the interpreters of that love. Thus they will fulfil their task with human and Christian responsibility.[3]

The Church also considers children "the supreme gift of marriage" who "contribute to the highest degree to their parents' welfare."[4] While bringing children into the world and educating them is a responsibility and hard work, it is also the greatest joy any couple can know. You are your parents' greatest joy. From the moment you were born, you have brought laughter and light and wisdom into their lives. Every parent is a better person because of the gift of their children. And someday, if God calls you to marriage, you may discover this in a whole new way through your own children.

Because the fruitfulness of human marriage images the fruitfulness of divine love and because the ability to bring forth life is such a sacred task and responsibility, it is always a grave sin to intentionally render the marital act sterile. That is, it is a grave sin to use any form of artificial contraception—both barrier and hormonal methods—or to permanently sterilize one or both of the spouses—through a vasectomy, tubal ligation, or hysterectomy—with the specific intention of preventing new life from coming to being.

God's love is always life-giving. He never holds anything back in the exchange of life and love that is the Holy Trinity. Nor does Christ ever hold anything back from his Church. He never says, "Today, I won't heal you. Today, I won't forgive you. Today, I won't feed you with my Body

---

[3] Pastoral Constitution on the Church in the Modern World *Gaudium et Spes* (December 7, 1965), §50.

[4] HV §9.

and Blood." Similarly, we are called to never hold anything back from our spouse. To give our heart and body but not our fertility—our God-given ability to bring new life into the world—is to only give part of ourselves. It makes the self-gift in marriage partial, not whole. And it corrupts the sign of divine love that God made marriage to be.

Natural Family Planning

That's not to say God expects every single act of married love to result in a baby. He doesn't. He didn't design the body that way. Because God doesn't expect that, neither does the Church. The Church leaves it up to each couple to prayerfully discern the number of children God is calling them to have. Couples are then free to welcome children as they come or space them using Natural Family Planning (NFP).

God actually created the female body so that it's only fertile for a small portion of the month. If, for serious reasons, a couple feels that they cannot handle a baby at the present moment or if unchanging health problems dictate they can have no more children, they can choose to abstain from marital relations during, immediately before, and immediately after ovulation. Typically, this means eight days of abstinence a month, although for some couples it can be more, especially following the birth of a child or for women with complicated cycles.

Different methods of Natural Family Planning help couples to track and monitor the woman's cycle by pinpointing ovulation using various signs of fertility. These methods are scientifically based and, when used correctly, are typically as effective as most major types of contraception.[5]

---

[5] For example, the journal for the Association of Family Physicians reported in 2012 that when the two primary signs of female fertility (cervical mucus and body temperature) are tracked, couples experience only a 0.4 percent chance of failure with perfect use and 7.5 percent chance of failure with typical use. That well exceeds the reliability of the condom (2 percent chance of failure with perfect use; 18 percent chance with typical use); the sponge (20 percent chance of failure with perfect use; 24 with typical use); and diaphragms (6 percent perfect; 12 percent typical). It also is statistically equivalent to the failure rate of oral contraceptives, the patch, the NuvaRing, and Depo-Provera injections (0.3 percent perfect; 6–9 percent typical). Crista B. Warniment and Kirsten Hansen, "Is Natural Family Planning a Highly Effective Method of Birth Control? Yes: Natural Family Planning Is Highly Effective and Fulfilling," *American Family Physician*,

Natural Family Planning does require things that contraception doesn't, though—namely communication and virtue, which is why so few couples use it when they feel like they need to avoid pregnancy. In order for it to be effective, couples have to talk openly and honestly with each other about the reasons they do or don't want another baby at the present moment. For some couples, that level of communication is difficult. NFP also requires that couples have discipline, self-control, humility, and trust in God's will (because nothing is 100 percent effective, including NFP). And NFP asks spouses to put the good of the marriage (and the physical and mental health of the wife) over their own physical desires.

When those virtues aren't there—when one or both of the spouses are selfish, immature, lustful, fearful, anxious, vain, or proud—NFP shines a light on those weaknesses. It illuminates where each spouse still needs to grow. And seeing those weaknesses can be hard.

NFP isn't easy. If it were, everyone would be doing it. Every single form of hormonal contraception, after all, comes with a host of unpleasant side effects, from mood swings and weight gain to acne, infertility, cancer, and even death. The World Health Organization classifies the hormonal birth control pill as a "class one carcinogen." That's the same classification it gives to cigarettes, and it's deserved. Studies show that oral contraceptives increase the risk of breast cancer by an estimated 20 percent and cervical cancer by 10–200 percent, depending on the length of use.[6]

There are more than just physical dangers to contraceptives, of course. When Pope Paul VI reiterated the Church's ancient teaching against contraception and sterilization in his 1968 encyclical *Humanae Vitae*, the oral contraceptive pill had just come on the market. The pope predicted that with its widespread use, an increase in divorce, promis-

---

November 15, 2012, https://www.aafp.org/afp/2012/1115/od1.html; Association of Reproductive Health Professionals, "Contraceptive Failure Rates," June 2014, http://www.arhp.org/Publications-and-Resources/Quick-Reference-Guide-for-Clinicians/choosing/failure-rates-table.

6 National Cancer Institute, "Oral Contraceptives and Cancer Risk," February 22, 2018, https://www.cancer.gov/about-cancer/causes-prevention/risk/hormones/oral-contraceptives-fact-sheet.

cuity, adultery, out-of-wedlock births, pornography, abortion, and the mistreatment of women would follow. He was right. Easy, effective contraception separated the procreative (babies) and unitive (bonding) aspects of the marital act. It made it easier for men to use women, easier to cheat, easier to end relationships.

Hormonal contraception also put the burden on the woman. She had to be the one willing to take on all the dangerous side effects of altering her natural body chemistry. She had to be the one to endure the mood swings, the weight gain, the discomfort. She, ultimately, had to be the one responsible for denying new life and putting her body at risk.

In contrast, Natural Family Planning puts the burden on both the man and woman. Both must communicate. Both must care more about the good of the other, the marriage, and the family than they care about their own desires. Both must grow in virtue in order to practice it. Accordingly, because of NFP's ability to show spouses where they need to grow and give them an opportunity for practicing virtue and better communication, NFP can, when approached with the right attitude, help strengthen marriages. It is, in many ways, not only an effective way to space or avoid births but the antidote to the very attitudes of selfishness that contraception encourages.

Infertility & Artificial Reproductive Technology

NFP is not just about avoiding pregnancy, though. It also can be used to achieve pregnancy. One in eight couples struggle to conceive and carry a baby to term. Natural Family Planning, paired with innovative fertility treatments such as NaProTECHNOLOGY can help couples achieve their dreams of bringing new life into the world in ethically sound ways.

Sometimes, though, nothing a couple does can help them get pregnant. This is a sorrow that the Bible recounts numerous times, in the stories of Hannah, Rachel, and John the Baptist's mother, Elizabeth. Tradition tells us that St. Joachim and St. Anne, the parents of the Blessed Virgin Mary, also struggled with infertility for decades before their very special daughter was born.

Infertility is one of the greatest crosses a couple can carry. Like any illness, it is a consequence of the fall. It is a symptom of brokenness. When couples can't conceive a child, something is broken in their bodies, either due to disease or age. The Church feels tremendous sympathy for couples who carry this cross, acknowledging in the Catechism that "couples who discover that they are sterile suffer greatly" (CCC 2374). The Church also urges scientists to pursue "research aimed at reducing human sterility . . . on condition that it is placed 'at the service of the human person, of his inalienable rights, and his true and integral good according to the design and will of God' [CDF, *Donum vitae intro.,* 2]" (CCC 2375).

In-vitro fertilization (IVF), almost every form of intrauterine insemination (IUI), and surrogacy do not meet those criteria. They are counter to the good of the human person and violate human dignity. Although those reproductive technologies can help produce a truly good end—a child—the means they use to reach that end are not good. IVF, surrogacy, and (sometimes) IUI involve a third person (an egg donor, sperm donor, or surrogate) in what is supposed to be a loving act between husband and wife. They almost always require the husband to engage in an act of self-abuse (masturbation), and IVF and surrogacy in particular have led to the destruction of millions of innocent lives.

Over the past forty years, one million children have been born through IVF. But for every baby born through IVF, fifteen embryos have either been thrown away, frozen, handed over for research, or died in utero, often through selective abortion. In the United States alone, more than four hundred thousand human embryos—human persons in one of the earliest stages of human life—remain frozen in storage facilities, abandoned by the parents and doctors who created them.[7]

Although the Church sympathizes with the deep pain of infertility, it urges married couples to remember that there are worse things than not being able to carry a child—namely, being outside of God's will. The Catechism states:

---

[7] Steve Doughty, "1.7 Million Embryos Created for IVF Have Been Thrown Away," *Daily Mail,* December 30, 2012, http://www.dailymail.co.uk/news/article-2255107/1-7-million-embryos-created-IVF-thrown-away-just-7-cent-lead-pregnancy.html.

A child is not something *owed* to one, but is a *gift*. The "supreme gift of marriage" is a human person. A child may not be considered a piece of property, an idea to which an alleged "right to a child" would lead. In this area, only the child possesses genuine rights: the right "to be the fruit of the specific act of the conjugal love of his parents," and "the right to be respected as a person from the moment of his conception" [CDF *Donum vitae* II, 8]. (CCC 2378)

Instead of pursuing illicit means to conceive, the Church first urges couples to seek treatment for the underlying cause of the infertility, many of which can be treated with surgery or medication. When that fails, she reminds couples that although their bodies may be infertile, their love doesn't have to be.

The Gospel shows that physical sterility is not an absolute evil. Spouses who still suffer from infertility after exhausting legitimate medical procedures should unite themselves with the Lord's Cross, the source of all spiritual fecundity. They can give expression to their generosity by adopting abandoned children or performing demanding services for others. (CCC 2379)

Through offering up their suffering and joining it to Christ's, adopting or fostering a child in need of a home, or simply exercising spiritual parenthood by serving others, couples' marriages can be fruitful. Likewise, all couples, fertile or infertile, with many children, few children, or none at all, are called to bear spiritual fruit, not just physical fruit in the world. This is why Holy Matrimony is classified as a "sacrament at the service of communion" (CCC 1211). Like Holy Orders, it is a sacrament "directed towards the salvation of others," and the more married couples help others on their journey to Christ, the more they are helped on their own journey (CCC 1534).

SELECTED READING
Pope St. Paul VI, Encyclical Letter on the Regulation of
Birth *Humanae Vitae* (July 25, 1968), nos. 8–13

Married love particularly reveals its true nature and nobility when
we realize that it takes its origin from God, who "is love," the Father
"from whom every family in Heaven and on earth is named."

Marriage, then, is far from being the effect of chance or the
result of the blind evolution of natural forces. It is in reality the wise
and provident institution of God the Creator, whose purpose was
to effect in man His loving design. As a consequence, husband and
wife, through that mutual gift of themselves, which is specific and
exclusive to them alone, develop that union of two persons in which
they perfect one another, cooperating with God in the generation
and rearing of new lives.

The marriage of those who have been baptized is, in addition,
invested with the dignity of a sacramental sign of grace, for it represents the union of Christ and His Church.

In the light of these facts the characteristic features and exi-
gencies of married love are clearly indicated, and it is of the highest
importance to evaluate them exactly.

This love is above all fully human, a compound of sense and
spirit. It is not, then, merely a question of natural instinct or emotional drive. It is also, and above all, an act of the free will, whose trust
is such that it is meant not only to survive the joys and sorrows of
daily life, but also to grow, so that husband and wife become in a way
one heart and one soul, and together attain their human fulfillment.

It is a love which is total—that very special form of personal
friendship in which husband and wife generously share everything,
allowing no unreasonable exceptions and not thinking solely of their
own convenience. Whoever really loves his partner loves not only for
what he receives, but loves that partner for the partner's own sake,
content to be able to enrich the other with the gift of himself.

Married love is also faithful and exclusive of all other, and this
until death. This is how husband and wife understood it on the day

on which, fully aware of what they were doing, they freely vowed themselves to one another in marriage. Though this fidelity of husband and wife sometimes presents difficulties, no one has the right to assert that it is impossible; it is, on the contrary, always honorable and meritorious. The example of countless married couples proves not only that fidelity is in accord with the nature of marriage, but also that it is the source of profound and enduring happiness.

Finally, this love is fecund. It is not confined wholly to the loving interchange of husband and wife; it also contrives to go beyond this to bring new life into being. "Marriage and conjugal love are by their nature ordained toward the procreation and education of children. Children are really the supreme gift of marriage and contribute in the highest degree to their parents' welfare."

Married love, therefore, requires of husband and wife the full awareness of their obligations in the matter of responsible parenthood, which today, rightly enough, is much insisted upon, but which at the same time should be rightly understood. Thus, we do well to consider responsible parenthood in the light of its varied legitimate and interrelated aspects.

With regard to the biological processes, responsible parenthood means an awareness of, and respect for, their proper functions. In the procreative faculty the human mind discerns biological laws that apply to the human person.

With regard to man's innate drives and emotions, responsible parenthood means that man's reason and will must exert control over them.

With regard to physical, economic, psychological and social conditions, responsible parenthood is exercised by those who prudently and generously decide to have more children, and by those who, for serious reasons and with due respect to moral precepts, decide not to have additional children for either a certain or an indefinite period of time.

Responsible parenthood, as we use the term here, has one further essential aspect of paramount importance. It concerns the objective moral order, which was established by God, and of which a right conscience is the true interpreter. In a word, the exercise of responsible parenthood requires that husband and wife, keeping a right order of priorities, recognize their own duties toward God, themselves, their families and human society.

From this it follows that they are not free to act as they choose in the service of transmitting life, as if it were wholly up to them to decide what is the right course to follow. On the contrary, they are bound to ensure that what they do corresponds to the will of God the Creator. The very nature of marriage and its use makes His will clear, while the constant teaching of the Church spells it out. . . .

Men rightly observe that a conjugal act imposed on one's partner without regard to his or her condition or personal and reasonable wishes in the matter, is no true act of love, and therefore offends the moral order in its particular application to the intimate relationship of husband and wife. If they further reflect, they must also recognize that an act of mutual love which impairs the capacity to transmit life which God the Creator, through specific laws, has built into it, frustrates His design which constitutes the norm of marriage, and contradicts the will of the Author of life. Hence to use this divine gift while depriving it, even if only partially, of its meaning and purpose, is equally repugnant to the nature of man and of woman, and is consequently in opposition to the plan of God and His holy will. But to experience the gift of married love while respecting the laws of conception is to acknowledge that one is not the master of the sources of life but rather the minister of the design established by the Creator. Just as man does not have unlimited dominion over his body in general, so also, and with more particular reason, he has no such dominion over his specifically sexual faculties, for these are concerned by their very nature with the generation of life, of which God is the source. "Human life is sacred—all men must recognize that fact," Our predecessor Pope John XXIII recalled. "From its very inception it reveals the creating hand of God."

QUESTIONS FOR REVIEW

1. What are the four elements of marriage in the New Covenant?
2. What does a person give in marriage?
3. Name four ways that a person can violate fidelity in marriage.
4. What does an annulment mean?
5. How, besides bringing children into the world, can a marriage be fruitful?

QUESTIONS FOR DISCUSSION

1. How has divorce touched your life? What effects have you seen come from divorce?
2. Have you ever thought about how many children you might have? How has your idea of family size been shaped by the culture? Why might this be a problem?
3. What in the Church's teachings about marriage appeals to you? What doesn't appeal to you? Why?

Chapter 3

THE SACRAMENT OF HOLY MATRIMONY

The Celebration of the Sacrament

For Catholics, a wedding ceremony is so much more than a precursor to a fancy party. It's also more than a mere exchange of vows before a minister. For Catholics, marriage is a sacrament. It is an occasion for God's grace breaking into human history and transforming the world. That transformation starts with the man and woman who are being married.

All sacraments are efficacious signs. They don't just signify spiritual realities; they also give the grace to make what they signify a reality. Marriage is the sign of Christ's relationship with his Church. It gives couples the grace they need to be as intimately united in spirit to each other as Christ is to his Church and, through their union, bear witness to the union of Christ and the Church.

Accordingly, the fitting way to celebrate the sacrament, which bestows such tremendous grace on a couple, is not on a beach, in a garden, or jumping out of a plane, but rather in a church, surrounded by witnesses, and with a liturgical celebration, preferably the Mass (but occasionally just the Liturgy of the Word).

The Catechism states:

In the Eucharist the memorial of the New Covenant is realized, the New Covenant in which Christ has united himself for ever to the Church, his beloved bride for whom he gave himself up [cf. LG 6]. It is therefore fitting that the spouses should seal their consent to give themselves to each other through the offering of their own lives by uniting it to the offering of Christ for his Church made present in the Eucharistic sacrifice, and by receiving the Eucharist so that, communicating in the same Body and the same Blood of Christ, they may form but "one body" in Christ [cf. 1 Cor 10:17]. (CCC 1621)

In the Latin rite, the ministers of the Sacrament of Holy Matrimony aren't the priest or the deacon, but rather the husband and wife. They confer the sacrament on each other through their mutual consent. That consent must be witnessed by a priest or deacon and at least two other people for validity. In the Eastern rite, the minister of the sacrament is the priest or bishop, who confers the sacrament on the couple through a special blessing.

In both rites the consent of the couple remains of absolute importance. Both the man and woman must freely agree to marry the other. They cannot agree to the marriage under duress or pressure from any outside influence. It must be their own free choice. It is that choice, the Church's canon law teaches, that "makes marriage."[1] The Catechism further explains the meaning of consent:

The consent consists in a "human act by which the partners mutually give themselves to each other": "I take you to be my wife"—"I take you to be my husband" [GS 48 §1; OCM 45; cf. CIC, can. 1057 §2]. This consent that binds the spouses to each other finds its fulfillment in the two "becoming one flesh" [Gen 2:24; cf. Mk 10:8; Eph 5:31]. (CCC 1627)

---

[1] Code of Canon Law (Washington, DC: Libreria Editrice Vaticana, 1983), can. 1057.

During the liturgy, both the man and the woman are asked three questions by the celebrant:

1. *Have you come here freely and without reservation to give yourselves to each other in marriage?*
2. *Will you honor each other as man and wife for the rest of your lives?*
3. *Will you accept children lovingly from God and bring them up according to the law of Christ and his Church?*

All three questions must be answered with a "yes," or the marriage cannot take place.

Next, the couple exchanges vows. While it has become standard in our secular culture for couples to write their own vows, the Church does not permit this. God is the author of marriage, not men, and so it is to his design of marriage that the spouses must consent. In the Latin rite, there are two forms of approved vows:

I, (name), take you, (name), to be my wife/husband. I promise to be true to you in good times and in bad, in sickness and in health. I will love you and honor you all the days of my life.

Or

I, (name), take you, (name), for my lawful wife/husband, to have and to hold, from this day forward, for better, for worse, for richer, for poorer, in sickness and in health, until death do us part.

Marriage is, in many senses, a sacrament of unity. It images the union of Christ and his Church, and it brings about the sacramental union of the spouses, making them spiritually "one flesh." For this reason, Catholics are always encouraged to marry other Catholics. Marrying someone who is not Catholic ("difference of confession") or not Christian ("disparity of cult") introduces disunity into the heart of the marriage.

Differences about faith and the very notion of marriage, but also different religious mentalities, can become sources of tension in marriage, especially as regards the education of children. The temptation to religious indifference can then arise. (CCC 1634)

Despite these concerns, the Church allows Catholics to marry non-Catholics under certain conditions. In the case of a Catholic marrying a baptized (but non-Catholic) Christian, the permission of the local ecclesiastical authority must be obtained. In the case of marrying a non-Christian, the Catholic spouse must receive an express dispensation from what is otherwise considered an impediment to marriage. In both cases, the Catholic must ensure that the non-Catholic spouse understands the ends of marriage and assents to the Catholic spouse both continuing to practice their faith and to raising any children they have in the Church.

Always, however, the hope of the Church is that through the love and witness of the Catholic spouse, true spiritual unity will eventually come to the marriage. The Catechism states:

> In marriages with disparity of cult the Catholic spouse has a particular task: "For the unbelieving husband is consecrated through his wife, and the unbelieving wife is consecrated through her husband" [1 Cor 7:14]. It is a great joy for the Christian spouse and for the Church if this "consecration" should lead to the free conversion of the other spouse to the Christian faith [cf. 1 Cor 7:14]. Sincere married love, the humble and patient practice of the family virtues, and perseverance in prayer can prepare the non-believing spouse to accept the grace of conversion. (CCC 1637)

Preparing for the Sacrament

As with the vocations of the priesthood and religious life, preparation for the Sacrament of Holy Matrimony begins early in life, in the home.

This is called "remote preparation." From the marriages that surround us when we're young—the marriages of our parents, grandparents, aunts, uncles, and family friends—we learn what it means to give oneself, to love another, and to live a life in union with another.

In our childhood home, we also form habits—habits of how we communicate love, disappointment, frustration, anger, pride, and concern, habits of how we resolve conflict, habits of how we show affection, spend money, prioritize time, interact with children, pursue our work, and approach chores. When these habits are healthy, they make it easier for us to have a healthy, happy marriage. When the habits aren't healthy, they can make it difficult for us to enter into marriage, or they can become a source of conflict or difficulty when we are married. The better habits our childhood home life helps us acquire, the better remote preparation for marriage we are receiving.

The next step in preparing for the Sacrament of Holy Matrimony is called "proximate preparation." This is the stage you are entering into now. Learning about the nature of marriage and its challenges, learning to have healthy friendships with members of the opposite sex, growing in chastity and the other virtues, and beginning to pray about the vocation God might be calling you to are all important aspects of preparing for marriage. So too is learning more about yourself: what makes you happy, what makes you feel fulfilled, what are your strengths, weaknesses, and areas of woundedness. The more time you spend learning these things now, the more readily you'll be able to enter into the vocation to which God calls you and the more joyfully you'll be able to live that vocation.

The third and final stage of preparation for marriage is called "immediate preparation." This begins once you are engaged to be married. Before you start picking out a dress or a wedding venue, the Church asks you first to go to your parish or parents' parish and work with the pastor there to set a date for the wedding. The pastor will meet with you and determine that you are both free to marry in the Church.

Additional preparation varies from diocese to diocese, but in most places, you will either attend a retreat or classes for engaged couples or meet regularly with a priest, deacon, or experienced married couple to talk more about the nature of marriage, your expectations of marriage, and challenges you might face as a couple. This preparation is especially important for couples who grew up in broken homes or homes where the marriage was not lived out in a healthy way. It ensures that you are aware of what marriage entails: the full and free gift of self, lifelong fidelity, and openness to children. It also will help you grow in knowledge of yourself and your spouse and equip you for some of the practical challenges you will face.

While this formal preparation process can, for some, feel unnecessary or even annoying, it is a critical part of a couple's journey to marriage. Reflecting on its importance, Pope Francis says:

> The call to married life, therefore, requires a heartfelt discernment of the quality of the relationship and a period of engagement to confirm it. To approach the Sacrament of Marriage, the engaged couple must establish the certainty that the hand of God is in their bond and that he precedes and accompanies them and will enable them to say: *With the Grace of Christ I promise to be faithful to you always.* They cannot promise each other fidelity *"in good times and in bad, in sickness and in health,"* and to love and honour one another all the days of their lives, solely on the basis of good will or of the hope that it 'will work out.' They need to ground themselves on the solid terrain of God's faithful Love. And this is why, before receiving the Sacrament of Matrimony, there should be a careful preparation, I would say a catechumenate, because with love one's entire life is at stake, and one does not kid around with love.[2]

Effects of the Sacrament

Remember what we talked about earlier—how humanity's fall from

---

[2] Pope Francis, Wednesday General Audience (October 24, 2018), available at http://w2.vatican.va/content/francesco/en/audiences/2018/documents/papa-francesco_20181024_udienza-generale.html.

grace made it difficult to live God's plan for marriage? Well, that remains true, even after Jesus' coming. He may have transformed human marriage in the New Covenant, making it into a holy sacrament and an image of his love for the Church, but loving our spouse as God intended us to love them is still hard. This is true for Christians and non-Christians alike, and it's why we see so many books and programs and therapists focused on helping people have better marriages.

All those "helps" can be effective (depending on what kind of help they're offering), but the very best help for living out God's plan for marriage is available only to baptized Christians who are validly married. This help is grace. And it comes to us through the Sacrament of Holy Matrimony.

Holy Matrimony, like every other sacrament, is an efficacious sign; it makes possible the thing it signifies. So, just as Baptism really does bring forgiveness for original sin and make us adopted children of God, marriage really does unite man and woman. It gives us grace that truly makes us "one flesh." That grace, as the Catechism explains, is

> intended to perfect the couple's love and to strengthen their indissoluble unity. By this grace they "help one another to attain holiness in their married life and in welcoming and educating their children" [LG 11 §2; cf. LG 41]. (CCC 1641)

This means that the grace of marriage gives us supernatural help to love our spouse, listen to our spouse, compromise with our spouse, respect our spouse, care for our spouse, be faithful to our spouse, support our spouse, suffer with our spouse, forgive our spouse, apologize to our spouse, and work with our spouse in raising a family and forming them in the faith. All that is difficult about marriage becomes easier with the help of grace.

This grace isn't just for the good of the marriage, though. It's also for our good. As we learn to love our spouse as Christ loved the Church, we become more Christlike. We become holier. The same goes for our spouse. Through loving and serving each other, in good times and bad, each spouse helps the other on their journey to holiness. This is one of the reasons why marriage is a vocation—a holy calling with supernatural dignity.

Marriage is also considered a "sacrament at the service of communion," which means the good it brings to the world is for more than just the spouses. The grace that couples receive through the Sacrament of Holy Matrimony enables them to rear and educate children with love and wisdom.

> The fruitfulness of conjugal love extends to the fruits of the moral, spiritual, and supernatural life that parents hand on to their children by education. Parents are the principal and first educators of their children [cf. GE 3]. In this sense the fundamental task of marriage and family is to be at the service of life. (CCC 1653)

The graces of marriage also help married couples serve the wider community—their extended families, neighbors, friends, the Church, and society.

> In our own time, in a world often alien and even hostile to faith, believing families are of primary importance as centers of living, radiant faith. For this reason the Second Vatican Council, using an ancient expression, calls the family the *Ecclesia domestica* [LG 11; cf. FC 21]. It is in the bosom of the family that parents are "by word and example . . . the first heralds of the faith with regard to their children. They should encourage them in the vocation which is proper to each child, fostering with special care any religious vocation" [LG 11]. (CCC 1656)

Challenges to Living the Sacrament

The grace of marriage gives couples so much help. It makes it possible for us to live marriage as God intended us to live it. But it doesn't make it easy. In a fallen world, living as God intended us to live will always be difficult. That's true for you right now as a student, and it will be true for you in another ten, twenty, or thirty years when you are living out whatever vocation God has for you.

Marriage in a Fallen World

Much of this difficulty is, in a sense, our own fault. Each of us is born with a tendency to sin ("concupiscence"), which means we each have certain weaknesses, parts of ourselves that aren't very good at resisting particular sins. Some of us are prone to pride. Others to vanity or lust or anger. Almost all of us are prone to selfishness. These weaknesses, if not addressed before marriage, affect our ability to love and be loved by our spouse.

Unlike in the movies, there is no such thing in this life as "happily ever after." All couples have to work at making and keeping a happy marriage. They have to continue growing in virtue, forgiving their spouses for their weaknesses and being forgiven for their own weaknesses. Some people don't want to do that work. They don't want to admit that they aren't perfect and still have growing and maturing to do. Or they are too afraid of letting go of bad habits, dangerous addictions, or hurtful ways of thinking. Or they're simply too broken to do the work marriage requires and never should have gotten married before first seeking healing. When this happens, marriages often fall apart, even marriages between two believing Catholics.

It's not just about us, though. For the past two thousand years, the human weaknesses of husband and wife have made living God's plan for marriage difficult. In the modern age, Catholic couples face a whole host of challenges from the culture, their friends, and even their families.

At the top of that list of challenges is divorce.

Marriage in a Culture of Divorce

As we discussed earlier, it is not a sin for one spouse to leave another in cases of abuse or endangerment. Likewise, sometimes people enter into a marriage not only unprepared to give themselves but truly unable to give themselves. The Church understands this and wants to support families that find themselves in these situations. Divorce is sometimes necessary. Annulments are granted for good reason. But a culture of divorce—where divorce is considered not just acceptable but good and normal—is a serious problem and a threat to the stability of all marriages.

First, this type of thinking changes how people approach marriage. It blinds people to the reality that marriage is supposed to be a lasting union—"until death do us part"—and many now enter into marriage without even really understanding what marriage is. "They say 'yes, for the rest of my life!' but they don't know what they are saying," Pope Francis has remarked.[3]

The ease with which divorce can be obtained, as well as its social acceptability, also prevents some people from putting the necessary work into their marriage. Forgiving another person is hard. Being faithful to another person is hard. Being vulnerable and changing deeply ingrained habits for another person—from how we communicate to how we fight, use technology, and clean our house—is hard. By comparison, divorce can appear easy. In a culture that supports divorce, just walking away from one's spouse often seems like the simplest way out of a difficult situation.

Most of all, since divorce has become so common, so too has growing up in a single-parent household. Many of us don't know what a healthy marriage looks like because we've never seen one up close. We don't know how a husband and wife can communicate in healthy ways, support one another, and care for one another because the people who were supposed to teach us that—our parents—couldn't do it themselves. This means we have to work extra hard to learn what healthy marriages look like so that we don't end up struggling in similar ways in our own marriages.

Moreover, even if our parents did have a strong marriage and we know what a healthy marriage looks like, that doesn't mean the person we marry will know the same. Many of us will end up marrying a person who comes from a broken family, which could mean that we will need to work

---

[3] Catholic News Agency, "Most Marriages Today Are Invalid, Pope Francis Suggests," June 16, 2016, https://www.catholicnewsagency.com/news/most-marriages-today-are-invalid-pope-francis-suggests-51752.

harder to help them overcome wounds from their family background, and that we will be marrying into a family whose dynamics aren't always healthy. Splitting holidays with multiple households, decades-old bitterness, unhealed wounds, and the loss of extended family ties—all of these things and more can put stress on even healthy and happy marriages.

Changing Ideas of Love and Family

In addition to the difficulties a culture of divorce can create for marriage, other cultural stressors can cause problems as well.

Thanks to the sexual revolution and hook-up culture, many people enter marriage with a history of previous sexual encounters and serious, almost marriage-like relationships. Wounds from those past relationships, habits of breaking up and looking for the next best thing, and unresolved feelings can make marriage difficult. So too can the increasingly common decision for couples to live together before marriage.

While many people think cohabitation will help them have a stronger marriage (reasoning that this way they'll know if they're truly compatible or not), the evidence doesn't bear this theory out. Couples who live together before they marry actually have a divorce rate that is 50 percent higher than those who don't.[4]

The widespread use of pornography is also an ever-present danger to marriage. Viewing pornography creates habits of seeing and treating another person as an object, often takes away one or both partners' desire for their spouse, and is always a serious sin, cutting off the flow of grace into one or both spouses' souls. The same holds true of abortion, contraception, and elective surgical sterilization. All are grievous sins, which not only change the couple's understanding of marriage but also kill (or wound) the life of God in each spouse's soul. That means the graces of marriage that couples need to live God's plan for marriage aren't flowing into their homes like they should be. Sin has, in effect, shut the door on that help.

---

[4] Julie Baumgardner, "Myths About Living Together," *First Things*, August 15, 2017, https://firstthings.org/myths-about-living-together.

Then there are the various attitudes coming at us from the media and entertainment industry about love and marriage. Pope Francis referenced this in 2016, when he told a group of young people, "Today there is a world war to destroy marriage. Today there are ideological colonisations which destroy, not with weapons, but with ideas."[5]

One of the places those ideas come to us is through movies. Romantic comedies can be fun and sweet, but they also can train us to think of marriage as a fairy tale, where all we need to do to live "happily ever after" is find our perfect match—someone devastatingly attractive, who always says and does the right thing, and never challenges us or frustrates us or disappoints us. But that person doesn't exist. We're all fallen human beings, which means, at some point, we'll all challenge, frustrate, and disappoint the person we love most.

Moreover, the person who might be the best spouse for us might not be the person who is good at saying or doing dashing and romantic things. The qualities that make for a good spouse—someone who is patient, helpful, supportive, and reliable—often don't make for the most interesting romantic comedy heroes and heroines. Not letting the culture shape our expectations for our spouse is a challenge we all face.

So too is rejecting the culture's message that marriage is all about you—what you get out of it, what you want, what you need. Loving another person as God wants us to love them demands that we die to ourselves and care more about our spouse's needs than we care about our own. It means sometimes we put others' dreams ahead of our own or that we let different dreams—dreams for our marriage, family, or children— take the place of old dreams. And it means that we think about marriage not in terms of what we can get out of it but rather in terms of what we can give to it—what we can give to our spouse, relationship, and family.

Importantly, marriage asks this of both spouses. It calls both husband and wife to sacrifice for each other, give to each other, and dream for each other. When just one spouse is doing all the sacrificing all the time, that

---

[5] Pope Francis, "Address to Priests, Religious, Seminarians, and Pastoral Workers," (October 1, 2016), available at http://w2.vatican.va/content/francesco/en/speeches/2016/october/documents/papa-francesco_20161001_georgia-sacerdo-ti-religiosi.html.

is a problem that needs addressing. Likewise, it doesn't mean that every dream you have for yourself has to die or be denied. It just means that pursuing those dreams needs to be evaluated and done in light of what is best for the marriage and the family. Some dreams will flourish in the context of family life and strengthen the family. Others might need to be set aside for a time or even let go. That reality may be difficult to accept for a person who thinks of marriage as a relationship ordered to their personal temporal happiness and not as a sacred calling ordered to the well-being of others and the eternal happiness of their souls.

The increasing practice of mixed marriages—marrying someone who doesn't share your Catholic Faith, your faith in Christ, or even your faith in God—can also set a marriage up to fail. Although this disparity in belief may not seem like a problem at the beginning of a relationship, when everything is easy and life seems like a love story, it can become a source of constant tension as the difficulties of life pile up. To not have a shared faith, a shared understanding of what matters most, and a shared belief in God's goodness and plan puts a marriage at a serious disadvantage from the start.

Finally, our current economic climate, which often demands that both husband and wife work outside the home, log long hours at the office or factory, commute long distances to work, accrue high amounts of debt to acquire an education or a home, and move far from family and friends adds layers of stress to modern marriages. All can leave couples feeling exhausted and anxious, with insufficient time to nourish their relationship and no support as they navigate both the demands of family life and the challenges of marriage.

* * *

So what is a Catholic couple to do? Looking at all the challenges that marriages face in our culture today, is a successful marriage even possible? How do any marriages withstand all these difficulties and challenges?

It comes back to grace. The more we make time with Jesus and prayer with our spouse a priority, the more the graces of the sacrament can be stirred up and strengthen our marriage. Likewise, the more we strive to grow in virtue, wisdom, and holiness, the more we'll be able to love our spouse as God calls us to love them. That means right now you can start doing the work in your soul that needs to be done in order for you to have a happy marriage. The closer you go to Jesus now, the more healing you seek out now, the more you grow in virtue now, and the more you establish healthy relationship patterns now, the better your chances are of entering into a happy, enduring Catholic marriage later on in life.

SELECTED READING
Pope St. John Paul II, Apostolic Exhortation on the Role of the Christian Family in the Modern World *Familiaris Consortio* (November 22, 1981), nos. 6–9

The situation in which the family finds itself presents positive and negative aspects: the first are a sign of the salvation of Christ operating in the world; the second, a sign of the refusal that man gives to the love of God.

On the one hand, in fact, there is a more lively awareness of personal freedom and greater attention to the quality of interpersonal relationships in marriage, to promoting the dignity of women, to responsible procreation, to the education of children. There is also an awareness of the need for the development of interfamily relationships, for reciprocal spiritual and material assistance, the rediscovery of the ecclesial mission proper to the family and its responsibility for the building of a more just society. On the other hand, however, signs are not lacking of a disturbing degradation of some fundamental values: a mistaken theoretical and practical concept of the independence of the spouses in relation to each other; serious misconceptions regarding the relationship of authority between parents and children; the concrete difficulties that the family itself experiences in the transmission of values; the growing number of divorces; the scourge of abortion; the ever more frequent recourse to sterilization; the appearance of a truly contraceptive mentality.

At the root of these negative phenomena there frequently lies a corruption of the idea and the experience of freedom, conceived not as a capacity for realizing the truth of God's plan for marriage and the family, but as an autonomous power of self-affirmation, often against others, for one's own selfish well-being.

Worthy of our attention also is the fact that, in the countries of the so-called Third World, families often lack both the means necessary for survival, such as food, work, housing and medicine, and the most elementary freedoms. In the richer countries, on the contrary, excessive prosperity and the consumer mentality, paradoxically joined to a certain anguish and uncertainty about the future, deprive married couples of the generosity and courage needed for raising up new human life: thus life is often perceived not as a blessing, but as a danger from which to defend oneself.

The historical situation in which the family lives therefore appears as an interplay of light and darkness.

This shows that history is not simply a fixed progression towards what is better, but rather an event of freedom, and even a struggle between freedoms that are in mutual conflict, that is, according to the well-known expression of St. Augustine, a conflict between two loves: the love of God to the point of disregarding self, and the love of self to the point of disregarding God.

It follows that only an education for love rooted in faith can lead to the capacity of interpreting "the signs of the times," which are the historical expression of this twofold love.

Living in such a world, under the pressures coming above all from the mass media, the faithful do not always remain immune from the obscuring of certain fundamental values, nor set themselves up as the critical conscience of family culture and as active agents in the building of an authentic family humanism.

Among the more troubling signs of this phenomenon, the Synod Fathers stressed the following, in particular: the spread of divorce and of recourse to a new union, even on the part of the faithful; the acceptance of purely civil marriage in contradiction to the vocation of the baptized to "be married in the Lord," the celebration of the marriage sacrament without living faith, but for other motives; the rejection of the moral norms that guide and promote the human and Christian exercise of sexuality in marriage.

The whole Church is obliged to a deep reflection and commitment, so that the new culture now emerging may be evangelized in depth, true values acknowledged, the rights of men and women defended, and justice promoted in the very structures of society. In this way the "new humanism" will not distract people from their relationship with God, but will lead them to it more fully.

Science and its technical applications offer new and immense possibilities in the construction of such a humanism. Still, as a consequence of political choices that decide the direction of research and its applications, science is often used against its original purpose, which is the advancement of the human person.

It becomes necessary, therefore, on the part of all, to recover an awareness of the primacy of moral values, which are the values of the human person as such. The great task that has to be faced today for the renewal of society is that of recapturing the ultimate meaning of life and its fundamental values. Only an awareness of the primacy of these values enables man to use the immense possibilities given him by science in such a way as to bring about the true advancement of the human person in his or her whole truth, in his or her freedom and dignity. Science is called to ally itself with wisdom.

The following words of the Second Vatican Council can therefore be applied to the problems of the family: "Our era needs such wisdom more than bygone ages if the discoveries made by man are to be further humanized. For the future of the world stands in peril unless wiser people are forthcoming."

The education of the moral conscience, which makes every human being capable of judging and of discerning the proper ways to achieve self-realization according to his or her original truth, thus becomes a pressing requirement that cannot be renounced.

Modern culture must be led to a more profoundly restored covenant with divine Wisdom. Every man is given a share of such Wisdom through the creating action of God. And it is only in faithfulness to this covenant that the families of today will be in a position to influence positively the building of a more just and fraternal world.

To the injustice originating from sin—which has profoundly penetrated the structures of today's world—and often hindering the family's full realization of itself and of its fundamental rights, we must all set ourselves in opposition through a conversion of mind and heart, following Christ Crucified by denying our own selfishness: such a conversion cannot fail to have a beneficial and renewing influence even on the structures of society.

What is needed is a continuous, permanent conversion which, while requiring an interior detachment from every evil and an adherence to good in its fullness, is brought about concretely in steps which lead us ever forward. Thus a dynamic process develops, one which advances gradually with the progressive integration of the gifts of God and the demands of His definitive and absolute love in the entire personal and social life of man. Therefore an educational growth process is necessary, in order that individual believers, families and peoples, even civilization itself, by beginning from what they have already received of the mystery of Christ, may patiently be led forward, arriving at a richer understanding and a fuller integration of this mystery in their lives.

QUESTIONS FOR REVIEW

1. In the Latin rite, who is considered the minister of the Sacrament of Holy Matrimony? What about in the Eastern rite?
2. What three promises does a couple make in a Catholic wedding liturgy?
3. What are the three stages of preparing for Holy Matrimony?
4. What does it mean that marriage is a "sacrament at the service of communion"?
5. What are the effects of the Sacrament of Holy Matrimony?

QUESTIONS FOR DISCUSSION

1. Why do you think the Church encourages Catholics to marry other Catholics? Can you think of a difference this might make in a marriage?
2. Do you want to be married? Why or why not?
3. What bad habits or wounds do you have now that might cause tension in a marriage someday? What could you start doing now to overcome those habits or wounds?

Part III

THE SACRAMENT OF
HOLY ORDERS

Jesus Christ is our one true high priest. He is "a high priest for ever according to the order of Melchiz'edek" (Heb 6:20). On the Cross, he offered the sacrifice of himself once and for all. United to Christ through Baptism, all the faithful have a share in his priesthood.

The Catechism explains:

> Christ, high priest and unique mediator, has made of the Church "a kingdom, priests for his God and Father" [Rev 1:6; cf. Rev 5:9–10; 1 Pet 2:5, 9]. The whole community of believers is, as such, priestly. The faithful exercise their baptismal priesthood through their participation, each according to his own vocation, in Christ's mission as priest, prophet, and king. Through the sacraments of Baptism and Confirmation the faithful are "consecrated to be . . . a holy priesthood" [LG 10 §1]. (CCC 1546)

On the night before he died, Jesus tasked his Apostles with carrying out his mission in the world in a special way. They were to proclaim the Gospel, celebrate the Eucharist, and care for the souls Christ had won for the Father. They were, in effect, to share in the eternal priesthood of Jesus Christ, continuing his mission on earth and signifying to the world his abiding presence in the Church.

Today, this mission continues to be carried out through those called to Holy Orders.

Chapter 1

The Nature of Holy Orders

Apostolic Succession

‖ Assigned Reading
Acts 1:13–26

Just as Jesus entrusted the continuation of his mission to the Apostles before his death, so too did the Apostles entrust their mission to others. Soon after Jesus' Ascension into heaven, they chose a successor for the Apostle who had been lost to sin: Judas Iscariot.

> And they put forward two, Joseph called Barsab'bas, who was surnamed Justus, and Matthi'as. And they prayed and said, "Lord, you know the hearts of all men, show which one of these two you have chosen to take the place in this ministry and apostleship from which Judas turned aside, to go to his own place." And they cast lots for them, and the lot fell on Matthi'as; and he was enrolled with the eleven apostles. (Acts 1:23–26)

Together, the twelve Apostles, under the headship of St. Peter, led the early Church. As Jesus commanded, they preached the Gospel, celebrated the sacraments, and governed the faithful. As the years passed, they also chose other men to succeed them and help them. They called their successors "bishops" and their helpers "presbyters" or priests (Phil 1:1; 1 Tim 3:1). They also chose men to help serve the material needs of the faithful—to ensure that all those who belonged to the Church had the food, clothing, and shelter they needed. These men they called "deacons" (Acts 6:1–7).

For the past two thousand years, this handing on of Christ's mission has continued through the Sacrament of Holy Orders.

The Three Degrees of Holy Orders

In the first century, St. Ignatius of Antioch, who was a disciple of the Apostle John, wrote:

> Let everyone revere the deacons as Jesus Christ, the bishop as the image of the Father, and the presbyters as the senate of God and the assembly of the apostles. For without them one cannot speak of the Church [St. Ignatius of Antioch, Ad Trall. 3,1: Sch 10, 96]. (CCC 1554)

Those words show us that since the very beginning of the Church, the Sacrament of Holy Orders has been conferred in three distinct degrees.

The Bishop

The Church's bishops are the successors to the Apostles. Their mission is the Apostles' mission. Their authority is the Apostles' authority. They "are regarded as transmitters of the apostolic line [LG 20]," and therefore they possess the *"fullness of the Sacrament of Holy Orders* . . . which, both in the liturgical tradition of the Church and the language of the Fathers of the Church, is called the high priesthood, the acme (*summa*) of the sacred ministry [LG 21 §2]" (CCC 1555, 1557).

Like Christ himself, each bishop is a "teacher, shepherd, and priest [LG 21]" (CCC 1558). In his diocese, as teacher, he has the authority to proclaim the Good News and teach the faith; as shepherd, he has the authority to govern his flock and administer the activities of the Church; and as priest, it is his sacred task to sanctify the people of God through the celebration of the sacraments. Each bishop wears a miter upon his head (a type of cap once worn by secular rulers in the first century and later adopted by the Church to signify the bishop's authority) and carries a crozier in his hand (a hooked staff which evokes a shepherd's crook), which both serve as signs of his authority.

In both the Latin and Eastern rite, the bishop is considered married to his diocese, just as Christ is married to the Church, and he wears a ring signifying that union. Although Eastern rite priests (and a select few Latin rite priests) are permitted to marry, bishops in both rites must always and everywhere be unmarried celibates, signifying the exclusivity of their devotion to the Church.

Today, the pope, in consultation with his advisors, chooses bishops. They must already be ordained priests. That hasn't always been the case, though, and in the early Church, bishops such as St. Ambrose found themselves unexpectedly elected to the episcopate directly by the people of their diocese, often before they were ordained and occasionally (as in Ambrose's case) before they were even baptized. Regardless, the bishop's authority to govern is contingent not on the people he serves but on his union with the college of bishops (all the bishops of the world) and his union with the pope. From among members of the College of Bishops, the pope also chooses archbishops (bishops of dioceses traditionally considered preeminent among a group of dioceses) or cardinals (a senior leader in the hierarchy who, among other duties, is tasked with helping elect the pope).

As the high priest of his diocese, only the bishop can celebrate all seven of the Church's sacraments. The ordination of priests is reserved to the bishop alone, and often, in the Latin Church, the Sacrament of Confirmation is also (although priests can, with the express permission of the bishop, confer the sacrament as well).

The Priest

Priests are the bishops' "co-workers," their helpers in teaching, governing, and sanctifying. As the Catechism explains, they act in the person of Christ, "*in persona Christi*," and are ordained "in order to preach the Gospel and shepherd the faithful as well as to celebrate divine worship *as true priests of the New Testament* [LG 28; cf. Heb 5:1–10; 7:24; 9:11–28; Innocent I, Epist. ad Decentium: PL 20, 554A; St. Gregory of Nazianzus, Oratio 2, 22: PG 35, 432B]" (CCC 1564).

Priests carry out a wide variety of tasks within the Church: teaching and preaching, administering and serving in parishes (only priests can serve as a parish's pastor), and serving in diocesan offices, helping to run the local Church. The heart of their ministry, however, is the celebration of the Eucharist. As the Catechism, quoting the Second Vatican Council, explains:

> "It is in the Eucharistic cult or in the *Eucharistic assembly* of the faithful (*synaxis*) that they exercise in a supreme degree their sacred office; there, acting in the person of Christ and proclaiming his mystery, they unite the votive offerings of the faithful to the sacrifice of Christ their head, and in the sacrifice of the Mass they make present again and apply, until the coming of the Lord, the unique sacrifice of the New Testament, that namely of Christ offering himself once for all a spotless victim to the Father" [LG 28; cf. Cor 11:26]. From this unique sacrifice their whole priestly ministry draws its strength [cf. PO 2]. (CCC 1566)

Unlike the bishops, whom they assist, priests cannot celebrate all seven sacraments. They cannot ordain other priests and, in the Latin rite, without the bishop's permission, they cannot celebrate Confirmation. Certain sins are also reserved to the bishop to forgive, including (but not limited to):

- Apostasy, heresy, schism
- Violation of consecrated bread and wine (the Body and Blood of Christ)
- Physical violence against a pope or bishop
- Unauthorized ordination of a bishop
- Direct violation by a confessor of the seal of Confession

- Revealing the overheard confession of another
- Attempted marriage by a religious or cleric
- Formal cooperation in an abortion

In most of these cases (but not all), the bishop can grant certain priests in his diocese permission to absolve the penitent, and Pope Francis did this for all priests, in 2016, regarding the sin of abortion.

Deacons

Unlike bishops and priests, the ministry of deacons is not described as a "priesthood." They are not able to offer the Eucharistic sacrifice or perform other priestly duties, so the term doesn't apply to them. They do have a share in the ecclesial ministry as the bishop's helpers, though, and are ordained for two primary purposes.

First, deacons assist the bishop and his priests in the celebration of the sacraments. Deacons in the Latin rite can be ministers of the Sacrament of Baptism, and assist in the celebration of the Eucharist and Holy Matrimony. They can proclaim the Gospel in the Church's liturgy, preach homilies, bless marriages, and preside at funerals. Deacons in the Eastern rite cannot be ministers of Baptism because the Eastern rite confers all three sacraments of initiation at the same time (Baptism, Eucharist, and Confirmation). Likewise, because in Eastern rite weddings the priest is the minister of the Sacrament of Holy Matrimony, the deacon cannot preside at these weddings.

Second, deacons carry out the ancient function of deacons in the Church: assisting with charitable service. In many dioceses, deacons run food pantries, homeless shelters, and other diocesan outreaches to the poor and needy. They also often visit the homebound, bringing the Eucharist to those who are sick, elderly, or unable to make it to Mass for other reasons.

Importantly, while deacons have existed in the Church since the first century (in Acts 6:5, we're told that St. Stephen, the Church's first martyr, was also one of the Church's first seven deacons), the Western Church at one point stopped ordaining men to the permanent diaconate.

That is, unlike the Eastern Church, which continued ordaining men to the deaconate for life, the Latin Church did not. They only ordained men to the transitional deaconate, meaning that the men would only serve as deacons for a short time (usually six months to a year) before they were ordained to the priesthood.

Today, the Church continues to ordain her candidates for the priesthood to the transitional deaconate but, since Vatican II, has reinstated the permanent deaconate, recognizing it as "an important enrichment for the Church's mission" in terms of its "liturgical and pastoral life" and "social and charitable works" (CCC 1571).

Spiritual Fathers

Ever since Jesus himself called the Twelve Apostles to continue his ministry on earth, the Church has clearly and without question understood that the Sacrament of Holy Orders could be conferred only on men. The most foundational reason for this is because that is what Jesus chose to do.

Although Jesus had many women among his close followers, although he appeared first to those women after his Resurrection, making them special bearers of the Good News, and although no one had a more important role in the redemption of humanity than the Blessed Mother, Jesus chose only men to be Apostles. He entrusted the continuation of his ministry—of teaching, governing, and celebrating the sacraments—only to men. His Apostles did the same. And their successors followed suit.

> The Lord Jesus chose men (*viri*) to form the college of the twelve apostles, and the apostles did the same when they chose collaborators to succeed them in their ministry [cf. Mk 3:14–19; Lk 6:12–16; 1 Tim 3:1–13; 2 Tim 1:6; Titus 1:5–9; St. Clement of Rome, Ad Cor. 42, 4; 44, 3: PG 1, 292–293; 300]. The college of bishops, with whom the priests are united in the priesthood, makes the college of the twelve an ever-present and ever-active reality until Christ's return. The Church recognizes herself to be bound by this choice made by the Lord himself. For this

reason the ordination of women is not possible [cf. John Paul II, MD 26–27; CDF, declaration, *Inter insigniores*: AAS 69 (1977) 98–116]. (CCC 1577)

Occasionally, to challenge this idea that only men can receive the Sacrament of Holy Orders, someone will reference St. Paul's Letter to the Romans, which mentions "Phoebe, a deaconess of the church at Cen'chre-ae" (Rom 16:1). But early Church documents make it clear that the role of deaconess was never thought of as one that had a share in the ministerial priesthood of Christ or the ecclesial ministry of the bishops. Both the Councils of Laodicea and Nicea, for example, explicitly state that deaconesses are lay persons. We also know from historical texts that deaconesses played a service role within the Church, performing tasks like assisting in the baptisms of women (which involved the catechumens stripping down completely) and overseeing other women's behavior during the liturgy.[1]

Why, though, would Jesus choose to exclude women?

Remember, in the Mass and in the Sacraments, the priest serves *in persona Christi*. He is an icon or a sign of Jesus Christ, the Bridegroom. The priest also exercises spiritual fatherhood. His task in the Church is like that of the man in the household: to be a father. And only men can be bridegrooms. Only men can be fathers.

As Catholics, we take the side of both faith and reason on questions of sex and gender.

Science tells us that a man is not just a man in appearance. Every single chromosome in his body is male. The same goes for women. A woman is not just a woman in her appearance. Every single chromosome in her body is female. Rarely, mutations occur. But that, like all other biological abnormalities—from holes in the heart to missing limbs—is a consequence of the fall, which introduced brokenness into the world. That is not to say that people born with these mutations are inherently

---

[1] See International Theological Commission, *From the Diakonia of Christ to the Diakonia of the Apostles* (2002), available at http://www.vatican.va/roman_curia/congregations/cfaith/cti_documents/rc_con_cfaith_pro_05072004_diaconate_en.html.

sinful, simply that genetic mutations themselves exist because of original sin.

On this matter, faith agrees with science. As Catholics, we know that God created us male and female, and we believe that the differences in our bodies go as deep as the soul. Both men and women are made in the image of God. But we image him in different ways. In this world, as John Paul II's *Theology of the Body* tells us, there are "two incarnations," "two ways . . . of being a body."[2] Both incarnations are important. Both "ways" matter. Each, in its own way, tells us something about the God that it images. The man reveals some truth about who God is to us. The woman reveals another truth about who God is. Fatherhood has one witness to give, motherhood another.

This means the masculine and feminine have eternal meaning and eternal importance. God created the human person this way for a reason, and the Church cannot change what he has established.

SELECTED READING
Second Vatican Council, Decree on the Ministry and Life of Priests *Presbyterorum Ordinis* (December 7, 1965), no. 2

The Lord Jesus, "whom the Father has sent into the world" (Jn 10:36) has made his whole Mystical Body a sharer in the anointing of the Spirit with which he himself is anointed. In him all the faithful are made a holy and royal priesthood; they offer spiritual sacrifices to God through Jesus Christ, and they proclaim the perfections of him who has called them out of darkness into his marvelous light. Therefore, there is no member who does not have a part in the mission of the whole Body; but each one ought to hallow Jesus in his heart, and in the spirit of prophecy bear witness to Jesus.

The same Lord has established ministers among his faithful to unite them together in one body in which, "not all the members have the same function" (Rom 12:4). These ministers in the society of

---

[2] TOB 10:1.

the faithful are able by the sacred power of orders to offer sacrifice and to forgive sins, and they perform their priestly office publicly for men in the name of Christ. Therefore, having sent the apostles just as he himself [had] been sent by the Father, Christ, through the apostles themselves, made their successors, the bishops, sharers in his consecration and mission. The office of their ministry has been handed down, in a lesser degree indeed, to the priests. Established in the order of the priesthood they can be co-workers of the episcopal order for the proper fulfillment of the apostolic mission entrusted to priests by Christ.

The office of priests, since it is connected with the episcopal order, also, in its own degree, shares the authority by which Christ builds up, sanctifies and rules his Body. Wherefore the priesthood, while indeed it presupposes the sacraments of Christian initiation, is conferred by that special sacrament; through it priests, by the anointing of the Holy Spirit, are signed with a special character and are conformed to Christ the Priest in such a way that they can act in the person of Christ the Head.

In the measure in which they participate in the office of the apostles, God gives priests a special grace to be ministers of Christ among the people. They perform the sacred duty of preaching the Gospel, so that the offering of the people can be made acceptable and sanctified by the Holy Spirit. Through the apostolic proclamation of the Gospel, the People of God are called together and assembled. All belonging to this people, since they have been sanctified by the Holy Spirit, can offer themselves as "a sacrifice, living, holy, pleasing to God" (Rom 12:1). Through the ministry of the priests, the spiritual sacrifice of the faithful is made perfect in union with the sacrifice of Christ. He is the only mediator who in the name of the whole Church is offered sacramentally in the Eucharist and in an unbloody manner until the Lord himself comes. The ministry of priests is directed to this goal and is perfected in it. Their ministry, which begins with the evangelical proclamation, derives its power and force from the sacrifice of Christ. Its aim is that "the entire commonwealth of the redeemed and the society of the saints be offered to God through the High Priest who offered himself also for us in his passion that we might be the body of so great a Head."

The purpose, therefore, which priests pursue in their ministry and by their life is to procure the glory of God the Father in Christ. That glory consists in this—that men working freely and with a grateful spirit receive the work of God made perfect in Christ and then manifest it in their whole lives. Hence, priests, while engaging in prayer and adoration, or preaching the word, or offering the Eucharistic Sacrifice and administering the other sacraments, or performing other works of the ministry for men, devote all this energy to the increase of the glory of God and to man's progress in the divine life. All of this, since it comes from the Pasch of Christ, will be crowned by the glorious coming of the same Lord, when he hands over the Kingdom to God the Father.

QUESTIONS FOR REVIEW

1. What are the three degrees of Holy Orders?
2. What are the three signs of a bishop's office, and what does each signify?
3. What sacraments can a priest celebrate?
4. Traditionally, what are the two primary duties of deacons?
5. Why does the Church teach that only men can be priests?

QUESTIONS FOR DISCUSSION

1. Have you ever known a priest or bishop who reminded you of Jesus? If so, why?
2. How have the priests and bishops you've known affected your faith, either for good or for ill? Explain.
3. Do you struggle with the Church's teaching that only men can be priests? Why or why not?

Chapter 2

The Sacrament of Holy Orders

Preparing for the Sacrament

Like all vocations, the first and most formative preparation anyone receives for a life of sacramental service to the Church comes through Christian families and communities. In the Second Vatican Council's "Decree on Priestly Training" (*Optatam Totius*), we're told:

> The principal contributors to this are the families which, animated by the spirit of faith and love and by the sense of duty, become a kind of initial seminary, and the parishes in whose rich life the young people take part. Teachers and all those who are in any way in charge of the training of boys and young men, especially Catholic associations, should carefully guide the young people entrusted to them so that these will recognize and freely accept a divine vocation. All priests especially are to manifest an apostolic zeal in fostering vocations and are to attract the interest of youths to the priesthood by their own life lived in a humble and industrious manner and in a happy spirit as well as by mutual priestly charity and fraternal sharing of labor.[1]

---

[1] Pope Paul VI, Decree on Priestly Training *Optatam Totius* (October 28, 1965), §2.

As a young man begins to suspect that he may have a call to the priesthood, he will be encouraged to discern that call with the help of a priest (often the diocesan vocations director). He will then begin the process of applying to seminary, either in his diocese or with a religious order. Some dioceses admit men to the formation process when they are still in high school and educate them at what are called "high school seminaries" or "minor seminaries." There also are "college seminaries" for young men who are college-aged. But most men don't enter seminary until they have graduated from college, and these days, increasing numbers enter seminary after spending several years (or more) working in the world at a secular job. The seminaries men attend after college are called "major seminaries."

Admission to seminary isn't automatic. Just as the young man has to discern his call, so too does the diocese or religious order. Admission to seminary is based on a belief that the young man is psychologically and spiritually healthy, shows an aptitude for priestly service, and that God may indeed be calling him to the priesthood.

Once in seminary, the discernment process continues. Under the care of seminary professors, spiritual directors, and the bishop, seminarians receive four types of formation: intellectual, spiritual, pastoral, and human. Intellectual formation is primarily what happens in the classroom, as the seminarians study philosophy and theology. Spiritual formation, under the direction of another priest, helps the seminarian mature as a man of prayer and grow in his relationship with Christ. Pastoral formation most often takes place out of the classroom—in parishes, schools, nursing homes, prisons, and other charitable ministries—and helps young men learn what is involved in the practical care of souls. Lastly, through it all, human formation focuses on helping the young man grow in the virtues and Christian maturity, overcoming vices and besetting sins, so that he can be a living witness to Christ in the world.

Throughout this process of formation, the seminarian continues to contemplate the promises he will make if he is ordained (typically after six years of upper-level college and postcollege formation). For diocesan priests, those promises are four in number.

First, he must promise obedience to his bishop. This is because every priest's ministry is a participation in his bishop's ministry. Priests are the bishop's co-workers, called to assist him in his sacred task of shepherding the Church. As the Catechism explains:

> Priests can exercise their ministry only in dependence on the bishop and in communion with him. The promise of obedience they make to the bishop at the moment of ordination and the kiss of peace from him at the end of the ordination liturgy mean that the bishop considers them his co-workers, his sons, his brothers and his friends, and that they in return owe him love and obedience. (CCC 1567)

Second, priests must promise to embrace simplicity. That is, they promise to renounce pursuing worldly careers and chasing after possessions, and instead focus their energies on serving God's people.

Third, priests promise to live a life of prayer. More specifically, they promise to pray the Liturgy of the Hours (also called the Divine Office) when they are ordained to the transitional deaconate, and then, during their ordination to the priesthood, they additionally promise to administer the sacraments and celebrate the Sacred Liturgy.

Lastly, priests in the Roman rite promise to remain celibate—to renounce marriage and physical intimacy "for the sake of the Kingdom of Heaven [Mt 19:12]" (CCC 1579). Priests of the Eastern rite who are already married do not have to commit to celibacy, but those who are unmarried at the time of their ordination to the priesthood do commit to living celibately for the remainder of their life.

Priests who are ordained for religious orders and institutes make additional vows. All take vows of poverty, chastity, and obedience (not just to their bishop but to the religious superiors in their order). Occasionally, an order may require an additional vow. The Jesuits, for example, also require their priests to take a vow of obedience to the pope.

In all this, explains Pope St. John Paul II in his post-synodal exhortation *Pastores Dabo Vobis*, "the Church in every age draws her inspiration from Christ's example." He continues:

In this sense, the "seminary" in its different forms—and analogously the "house" of formation for religious priests—more than a place, a material space, should be a spiritual place, a way of life, an atmosphere that fosters and ensures a process of formation, so that the person who is called to the priesthood by God may become, with the sacrament of orders, a living image of Jesus Christ, head and shepherd of the Church.[2]

Permanent Deacons and Bishops

Unlike transitional deacons, who go on to be ordained as priests, permanent deacons do not attend seminary. Most are married men who work in the world and have families to care for. Instead of spending upwards of six years in intensive preparation, as candidates for the priesthood do, candidates for the permanent deaconate attend ongoing formation classes through their diocese, where they receive intellectual, spiritual, pastoral, and human formation that is focused on the particular duties they will have as deacons.

Bishops in the Roman rite are chosen from among the priesthood. Bishops in the Eastern rite are chosen from among celibate monks. They receive no additional formal preparation for their duties, but rather are prepared through their years of prayer and service as a priest.

Celebration of the Sacrament

For a man to become a deacon, priest, or bishop, he must first be "ordained" by his bishop (or, for the ordination of a bishop, by several bishops). For all three degrees of Holy Orders, ordination takes place in the context of the Mass. After the conclusion of the readings, the candidates for ordination are called forward. The presiding bishop "accepts"

---

[2] Pope John Paul II, Post-Synodal Apostolic Exhortation on the Formation of Priests in the Circumstances of the Present Day *Pastores Dabo Vobis* (March 25, 1992), §42.

them for ordination, and the homily is preached. The bishop then "interrogates" the men, who affirm their readiness to assume the duties that will follow ordination and make the necessary promises. Next, the candidates lie prostrate before the altar, and the congregation calls upon the assistance of the saints by singing the Litany of the Saints.

After that, in the case of deacons, the candidate kneels before his bishop, and the bishop alone lays hands on the candidate's head while praying aloud over him. Following the prayer, an assisting deacon or priest puts a deacon's stole around the new deacon's neck and places a dalmatic (a vestment worn by deacons) on him. The newly ordained deacon once more kneels before the bishop, who places the Book of the Gospels into his hands and says, "Receive the Gospel of Christ, whose herald you now are. Believe what you read, teach what you believe, and practice what you teach." The ordination ceremony then ends with the kiss of peace, and the Mass continues with the Liturgy of the Eucharist.

The ordination of priests differs from that of deacons in that it's not just the bishop who lays hands on the candidate's head, but also all of the priests who are present that day. The bishop goes first, followed by the priests. The candidate then kneels before the bishop, who says a prayer of consecration over him. After that, the new priest is vested in a stole and chasuble (the vestment worn by priests during the liturgy). The bishop then anoints the new priest's hands with chrism oil, saying, "The Father anointed our Lord Jesus Christ through the power of the Holy Spirit. May Jesus preserve you to sanctify the Christian people and to offer sacrifice to God." The Mass continues with the presentation of the gifts and the presentation of the paten and chalice (holding the bread and wine to be consecrated) by the bishop to the newly ordained priest. The kiss of peace and the remainder of the Liturgy of the Eucharist follow.

For the ordination of a bishop, the Liturgy of the Word is followed by the reading of the Mandate of the Holy See confirming the ordination of the candidate. The ceremony then proceeds in a manner similar to that of deacons and priests, although when it comes to the laying on of hands, it is first done by the presiding bishop and then by all the other bishops concelebrating the Mass. Then, with the candidate kneeling, two deacons hold the open Book of the Gospels over his head while the presiding bishop prays the prayer of consecration aloud. It begins:

> God the Father of our Lord Jesus Christ, Father of mercies and
> God of all consolation, you dwell in Heaven, yet look with com-
> passion on all that is humble. You know all things before they
> came to be; by your gracious word you have established the plan
> of your Church. From the beginning you chose the descendants
> of Abraham to be your holy nation. You established rulers and
> priests, and did not leave your sanctuary without ministers to
> serve you. From the creation of the world you have been pleased
> to be glorified by those whom you have chosen.

The prayer then continues, with all the other bishops present joining in,
praying:

> So now pour out upon this chosen one the power that is from
> you, the governing Spirit whom you gave to your beloved Son,
> Jesus Christ, the Spirit given by him to his holy apostles, who
> founded the Church in every place to be your temple for the
> unceasing glory and praise of your name.

The presiding bishop then completes the prayer and anoints the
head of the new bishop, saying, "God has brought you to share the high
priesthood of Christ. May he pour out on you the oil of mystical anointing and enrich you with spiritual blessings." The Book of the Gospels
is next handed to the new bishop. After that, the presiding bishop puts
a ring on the new bishop's right hand, signifying his "marriage" to the
Church, as well as a miter on his head and a crozier in his hand. The new
bishop then takes a seat, and the Mass continues with the kiss of peace
and the Liturgy of the Eucharist.

Effects of the Sacrament

The Sacrament of Holy Matrimony makes the husband and wife spiritually "one flesh," but that union endures only as long as both spouses are alive; the marriage bond is broken by the death of one spouse. In contrast, the Sacrament of Holy Orders confers an enduring spiritual mark or "an indelible spiritual character" on the soul. That character enables the ordained to "act as a representative of Christ, Head of the Church, in his triple office of priest, prophet, and king" and it endures forever (CCC 1581). Even if, for grave reasons, the deacon, priest, or bishop is removed from his office and not permitted to function as a minister of the Church, the character of his ordination remains. "The vocation and mission received on the day of his ordination mark him permanently" (CCC 1583).

Importantly, because it is Christ who acts through the minister, the personal holiness of the deacon, priest, or bishop does not objectively prevent Christ from working through him. The sacraments celebrated by ministers in grave sin are still efficacious signs, giving grace to those who receive them. St. Augustine states:

> As for the proud minister, he is to be ranked with the devil. Christ's gift is not thereby profaned: what flows through him keeps its purity, and what passes through him remains clear and reaches the fertile earth. ... The spiritual power of the sacrament is indeed comparable to light: those to be enlightened receive it in its purity, and if it should pass through defiled beings, it is not itself defiled [St. Augustine, In Jo. ev. 5, 15: PL 35, 1422]. (CCC 1584)

Like marriage, though, the Sacrament of Holy Orders gives the minister the grace he needs to live out his vocation and perform the duties of his office. Configured by grace to Christ as Priest, Teacher, and Pastor, bishops, priests, and deacons each receive the grace proper to their role in the Church. For the bishop, the Catechism states:

This is first of all a grace of strength ("the governing spirit": Prayer of Episcopal Consecration in the Latin rite) [cf. *Roman Pontifical*, Ordination of Bishops 26, Prayer of Consecration; cf. CD 13; 16]: the grace to guide and defend his Church with strength and prudence as a father and pastor, with gratuitous love for all and a preferential love for the poor, the sick, and the needy. This grace impels him to proclaim the Gospel to all, to be the model for his flock, to go before it on the way of sanctification by identifying himself in the Eucharist with Christ the priest and victim, not fearing to give his life for his sheep. (CCC 1586)

Likewise, the words prayed during the rite of ordination for Byzantine priests express the graces conferred upon all priests by the sacrament:

Lord, fill with the gift of the Holy Spirit
him whom you have deigned to raise to the rank of the
    priesthood,
that he may be worthy to stand without reproach before your
    altar
to proclaim the Gospel of your kingdom,
to fulfill the ministry of your word of truth,
to offer you spiritual gifts and sacrifices,
to renew your people by the bath of rebirth;
so that he may go out to meet
our great God and Savior Jesus Christ, your only Son,
on the day of his second coming,
and may receive from your vast goodness
the recompense for a faithful administration of his order.

Finally, through their ordination, deacons receive the strength necessary to assist the bishop and his priests in the service of the liturgy, the proclamation of the Gospel, and works of charity.

As with marriage, the grace given through the Sacrament of Holy Orders is no guarantee against sin. The ordained minister can neglect those graces and reject them by breaking the promises made on the day of his ordination, choosing his will over God's, and failing to walk the difficult path to holiness. But when the minister clings to Christ and stirs up the graces of his ordination through prayer, sacrifice, and works of mercy, he not only can more effectively bear witness to the One to whom he is configured, but he also can more quickly and joyfully proceed along the path that leads to heaven.

SELECTED READING
Pope St. John Paul II, Post-Synodal Apostolic Exhortation on the Formation of Priests in the Circumstances of the Present Day *Pastores Dabo Vobis* (March 25, 1992), nos. 8–9

The many contradictions and potentialities marking our societies and cultures—as well as ecclesial communities—are perceived, lived and experienced by our young people with a particular intensity and have immediate and very acute repercussions on their personal growth. Thus, the emergence and development of priestly vocations among boys, adolescents and young men are continually under pressure and facing obstacles.

The lure of the so-called "consumer society" is so strong among young people that they become totally dominated and imprisoned by an individualistic, materialistic and hedonistic interpretation of human existence. Material "well-being," which is so intensely sought after, becomes the one ideal to be striven for in life, a well-being which is to be attained in any way and at any price. There is a refusal of anything that speaks of sacrifice and a rejection of any effort to look for and to practice spiritual and religious values. The all-determining "concern" for having supplants the primacy of being, and consequently personal and interpersonal values are interpreted and lived not according to the logic of giving and generosity but according to the logic of selfish possession and the exploitation of others.

This is particularly reflected in that outlook on human sexuality according to which sexuality's dignity in service to communion and to the reciprocal donation between persons becomes degraded and thereby reduced to nothing more than a consumer good. In this case, many young people undergo an affective experience which, instead of contributing to a harmonious and joyous growth in personality which opens them outward in an act of self-giving, becomes a serious psychological and ethical process of turning inward toward self, a situation which cannot fail to have grave consequences on them in the future.

In the case of some young people a distorted sense of freedom lies at the root of these tendencies. Instead of being understood as obedience to objective and universal truth, freedom is lived out as a blind acquiescence to instinctive forces and to an individual's will to power. Therefore, on the level of thought and behavior, it is almost natural to find an erosion of internal consent to ethical principles. On the religious level, such a situation, if it does not always lead to an explicit refusal of God, causes widespread indifference and results in a life which, even in its more significant moments and more decisive choices, is lived as if God did not exist. In this context it is difficult not only to respond fully to a vocation to the priesthood but even to understand its very meaning as a special witness to the primacy of "being" over "having," and as a recognition that the significance of life consists in a free and responsible giving of oneself to others, a willingness to place oneself entirely at the Service of the Gospel and the kingdom of God as a priest.

Often the world of young people is a "problem" in the Church community itself. In fact, if in them—more so than in adults—there is present a strong tendency to subjectivize the Christian faith and to belong only partially and conditionally to the life and mission of the Church, and if the Church community is slow for a variety of reasons to initiate and sustain an up-to-date and courageous pastoral care for young people, they risk being left to themselves, at the mercy of their psychological frailty, dissatisfied and critical of a world of adults who, in failing to live the faith in a consistent and mature fashion, do not appear to them as credible models.

Thus we see how difficult it is to present young people with a full and penetrating experience of Christian and ecclesial life and to educate them in it. So, the prospect of having a vocation to the priesthood is far from the actual everyday interests which young men have in life.

Nevertheless, there are positive situations and tendencies which bring about and nurture in the heart of adolescents and young men a new readiness, and even a genuine search, for ethical and spiritual values. These naturally offer favorable conditions for embarking on the journey of a vocation which leads toward the total gift of self to Christ and to the Church in the priesthood.

First of all, mention should be made of the decrease of certain phenomena which had caused many problems in the recent past, such as radical rebellion, libertarian tendencies, utopian claims, indiscriminate forms of socialization and violence.

It must be recognized, moreover, that today's young people, with the vigor and vitality typical of their age, are also bearers of ideals which are coming to the fore in history: the thirst for freedom; the recognition of the inestimable value of the person; the need for authenticity and sincerity; a new conception and style of reciprocity in the rapport between men and women; a convinced and earnest seeking after a more just, sympathetic and united world; openness and dialogue with all; and the commitment to peace.

The fruitful and active development among so many young people today of numerous and varied forms of voluntary service, directed toward the most forgotten and forsaken of our society, represents in these times a particularly important resource for personal growth. It stimulates and sustains young people in a style of life which is less self-interested and more open and sympathetic toward the poor. This way of life can help young men perceive, desire and accept a vocation to stable and total service of others, following the path of complete consecration to God as a priest.

The recent collapse of ideologies, the heavily critical opposition to a world of adults who do not always offer a witness of a life based on moral and transcendent values, and the experience of companions who seek escape through drugs and violence—contribute in no small fashion to making more keen and inescapable the fundamental question as to what values are truly capable of giving the fullest meaning to life, suffering and death. For many young people the question of religion and the need for spirituality are becoming more explicit. This is illustrated in the desire for "desert experiences" and for prayer, in the return to a more personal and regular reading of the word of God and in the study of theology.

As has happened in their involvement in the sphere of voluntary social service, young people are becoming more actively involved as leaders in the ecclesial community, above all through their membership in various groups—whether traditional but renewed ones or of more recent origin. Their experience of a Church challenged to undertake a "new evangelization" by virtue of her faithfulness to the Spirit who animates her and in response to the demands of a world far from Christ but in need of him, as well as their experience of a Church ever more united with individuals and peoples in the defense and promotion of the dignity of the person and of the human rights of each and every one—these experiences open the hearts and lives of the young to the exciting and demanding ideals which can find their concrete fulfillment in following Christ and in embracing the priesthood.

Naturally it is not possible to ignore this human and ecclesial situation—characterized by strong ambivalence—not only in the pastoral care of vocations and the formation of future priests, but also in the care of priests in their life and ministry and their ongoing formation. At the same time, while it is possible to detect various forms of "crisis" to which priests are subjected today in their ministry, in their spiritual life and indeed in the very interpretation of the nature and significance of the ministerial priesthood—mention must likewise be made, in a spirit of joy and hope, of the new positive possibilities which the present historical moment is offering to priests for the fulfillment of their mission.

QUESTIONS FOR REVIEW

1. What are the four dimensions of priestly formation?
2. With what vestment is the deacon clothed at his ordination? What is he given and why?
3. With what vestments is the priest clothed at his ordination? What is he given and why?
4. What are the effects of the Sacrament of Holy Orders for deacons? Priests? Bishops?
5. Does the holiness of the ordained man affect the efficacy of the sacraments he celebrates? Why or why not?

QUESTIONS FOR DISCUSSION

1. Why do you think priestly formation includes human formation? What does that phrase mean to you? Why do you think it matters so much for a priest?
2. Have you ever attended an ordination of any kind? If so, what impressed you the most about it?
3. The holiness of a priest doesn't affect the efficacy of the sacraments. Based on your own experience of Catholic parish life, why does the holiness of the priest still matter?

Part IV

The Consecrated Life

God made matter. God loves matter. And he uses matter to help us understand who he is and how he loves us. This is true of the sun, the mountains, and the sea, which communicate to us something of God's glory, majesty, and power. And it's true of the three permanent states in life to which he calls us.

Marriage helps us understand God's love for us, the life of the Trinity, and the relationship of Christ and his Church. Holy Orders helps us understand God's fatherly love, as well as Christ's eternal priesthood and total self-gift to the Church. And the consecrated life gives us a glimpse into the life we all hope to live in heaven, a life where love of God consumes our every moment and every part of our being. The consecrated life is what the Church calls an eschatological sign, reminding us that this life is not the end. It is passing. Our true home and true life is in heaven.

a glimpse of . . .

> Immersed in the things of the Lord, the consecrated person remembers that "here we have no lasting city" (Heb 13:14), for "our commonwealth is in Heaven" (Phil 3:20). The one thing necessary is to seek God's "Kingdom and his righteousness" (Mt 6:33), with unceasing prayer for the Lord's coming.[1]

---

[1] Pope John Paul II, Post-Synodal Apostolic Exhortation on the Consecrated Life and Its Mission in the Church and in the World *Vita Consecrata* (March 25, 1996), §26.

Chapter 1

THE NATURE AND FORMS OF CONSECRATED LIFE

The Evangelical Counsels

The Catechism defines the consecrated life as "The state of life which is constituted by the profession of the evangelical counsels [LG 44 §4]" (CCC 914). That is, everyone who enters the consecrated life makes permanent vows that bind them to the practice of poverty, chastity, and obedience.

The evangelical counsels aren't just for those living the consecrated life, though. Christ calls every one of his followers to somehow embrace poverty, chastity, and obedience.

Lay Catholics living in the world, both single and married, practice poverty when we give generously to the Church and those in need, as well as when we strive to live simply, according to our duties in life. Lay Catholics practice chastity when, as single people, we save sexual intimacy for marriage and when, as married people, we practice fidelity to our spouse and respect the Church's teachings on intimacy. Finally, lay Catholics practice obedience when we follow the Church's teachings and when spouses obey one another in love.

how Catholics practice

Likewise, those who have taken Holy Orders practice poverty by faithfully living their vow of simplicity. They practice chastity most often through embracing continence, but in the case of married priests, they practice chastity in a way similar to other married Catholics. And they practice obedience by honoring their vow of obedience to their bishop.

Jesus calls all of his followers to embrace these counsels because they help us to grow in the virtue of charity, which is the virtue that helps us to love as God loves. Unlike those living the vocations of marriage and Holy Orders, those living the vocation of consecrated life solemnly vow to dedicate themselves to practicing poverty, chastity, and obedience. Living those vows is the hallmark of their vocation. Likewise, growing in love for Christ is the focus of their entire life. As the Catechism states, for those living the consecrated vocation, "Christ's coming remains for all those consecrated both the origin and rising sun of their life" (CCC 933).

As such, for the rest of the Church, the consecrated person is "a special sign of the mystery of redemption" (CCC 932). The Catechism continues:

> To follow and imitate Christ more nearly and to manifest more clearly his self-emptying is to be more deeply present to one's contemporaries, in the heart of Christ. For those who are on this "narrower" path encourage their brethren by their example, and bear striking witness "that the world cannot be transfigured and offered to God without the spirit of the Beatitudes" [LG 31 §2]. (CCC 932)

The evangelical counsels and singular devotion to Christ are the hallmarks of every consecrated person's life. That being said, there are many different ways that someone wanting to live the consecrated life can pursue that vocation.

The Different Forms of Consecrated Life

Reflecting upon the many and varied forms of consecrated life, the Catechism describes the vocation as "one great tree with many branches," explaining:

"From the God-given seed of the counsels a wonderful and wide-spreading tree has grown up in the field of the Lord, branching out into various forms of the religious life lived in solitude or in community. Different religious families have come into existence in which spiritual resources are multiplied for the progress in holiness of their members and for the good of the entire Body of Christ" [LG 43]. (CCC 917)

Over the past two millennia, new forms of consecrated life have continually emerged, thrived, and (occasionally) receded. In the future, new forms of consecrated life will likely continue to emerge, as the needs of the Church and culture change. Currently, though, the primary forms of consecrated life around the world include eremitic life, monastic life, apostolic religious life, societies of apostolic life, secular institutes, consecrated virgins, and consecrated widows.

Forms of consecrated life

Eremitic Life

Those who live the eremitic life are commonly called "hermits," and this is the oldest known form of consecrated life in the Church. One of the first hermits on record was St. Anthony of Egypt, who, in the third century, walked away from his family's wealth to live a solitary life in the desert, pursuing holiness in silence through prayer, fasting, and other forms of penance. In the centuries that have followed, countless other men have followed suit, retreating entirely from the world and their fellow men in order to pursue Christ with a single-minded devotion.

Of hermits, the Catechism says:

They manifest to everyone the interior aspect of the mystery of the Church, that is, personal intimacy with Christ. Hidden from the eyes of men, the life of the hermit is a silent preaching of the Lord, to whom he has surrendered his life simply because he is everything to him. Here is a particular call to find in the desert, in the thick of spiritual battle, the glory of the Crucified One. (CCC 921)

Monastic Life

St. Anthony of Egypt sought solitude in the desert. For a while, he found it. But then, others began wanting what he had—not just a life of prayer in the desert but also his wisdom and guidance. So they began flocking to him, setting up camp around him, and asking for his help. St. Anthony eventually organized his new neighbors into a community with a shared goal of growing in holiness through prayer and fasting. For this reason, he is often called "the father of monasticism."

Three centuries after Anthony, another devout man named Benedict also tried to become a hermit but found himself similarly pursued by those wanting to learn from him. Eventually, he organized those followers into a community and wrote a rule for their community life. Known as the Rule of St. Benedict, it went on to inspire the establishment of countless monasteries for the next fourteen hundred years and shape their way of life, particularly in the West. (In the East, monastic life is guided primarily by a different rule, the Rule of St. Basil, which was written by the great Doctor of the Church, St. Basil of Caesarea.)

Both men and women can live the monastic life, although with the exception of some "double monasteries" that existed in the Middle Ages, monastic houses are always single sex. Men living this life are called monks. The women are called nuns.

The primary goal of the monastic life is contemplation, with the monks and nuns dividing their time between work (such as cooking, farming, making items to sell in order to support the monastery, or scholarship) and prayer. In addition to the daily celebration of the Mass and private prayer, monks and nuns pray the Liturgy of the Hours.

In the centuries after the fall of the Roman Empire, monasteries were integral to preserving both sacred and secular knowledge, with both monks and nuns copying the Scriptures and great works of secular learning, as well as pursuing theological scholarship of their own. The first hospitals were established in monasteries, as a way for the monks and nuns to provide care to the poor and sick, and many of the first schools in Western Europe were established in monasteries as well.

Today, monks and nuns serve a critical role in the Church. Although their lives are primarily lived apart from the world, they remain engaged with the world through their prayers, penances, and the liturgies they celebrate. Each of us is blessed in ways we will never know, this side of heaven, by the contemplative ministry of those living the monastic life.

Apostolic Religious Life

During Christianity's first millennium, if you wanted to live the consecrated life in community, you lived in a monastery and stayed put. Most monks traveled little. Virtually no nuns traveled at all. This changed in the twelfth century with the Mendicant Orders. Under the leadership of men like St. Dominic and St. Francis of Assisi, consecrated men began moving about the world, going wherever their order determined the need was greatest, to preach and teach. They lived in community, but their mission field extended beyond their monastery or church. Their call was to engage the culture.

As the years passed, more orders, for both men (often "friars" or "brothers") and women ("sisters"), took on this missionary apostolate. They opened schools, hospitals, and orphanages, ministered to the poor and the elderly, and traveled across oceans to bring the Gospel to those who had never heard it. Called "active religious," these orders were instrumental in establishing the Church here in the United States. Today, that work continues, as "Religious life in its various forms is called to signify the very charity of God in the language of our time" (CCC 926).

Together with monastic or contemplative religious life, active religious life "is distinguished from other forms of consecrated life by its liturgical character, public profession of the evangelical counsels, fraternal life led in common, and witness given to the union of Christ with the Church [cf. CIC, cann. 607; 573; UR 15]" (CCC 925).

Societies of Apostolic Life

Societies of apostolic life are a form of consecrated life that has much in common with active religious life. Their members typically wear habits, live in community, and pursue a common purpose. That could be education, evangelization, serving the poor, caring for the sick, or another form of service.

Where these societies differ from religious orders, both active and contemplative, is that their members don't take public vows of poverty, chastity, and obedience. Instead, they "strive for the perfection of charity through the observance of the constitutions" of their society (CCC 930). These constitutions are essentially the rule of life laid out in the founding documents of their society. Societies of apostolic life also differ from religious orders in that community life, while important, is less important than the shared apostolate. This is why many of these societies were established in the first place: to give members greater flexibility in how they pursued their common apostolate.

Secular Institutes, Consecrated Virgins, and Consecrated Widows

Not all people living the consecrated vocation live in community and spend their lives serving their community. Some live and work in the world as consecrated individuals.

One way to do this is through a secular institute. Those who belong to one of the two hundred-plus secular institutes in the world profess the evangelical counsels of poverty, chastity, and obedience but strive for perfection in the world. Most of the institutes are primarily for lay people, but a few are designed specifically for priests. Those priests continue to serve their dioceses while also honoring their vows as a member of the secular institute.

Consecrated virgins and widows reflect the ancient practice of the Church, where either a woman who has never married or a woman who has been widowed can, under the authority of her bishop, consecrate herself exclusively to God's service. Both the virgin and the widow make a vow of poverty, obedience to their bishop, and either to remain in a state of virginity or to embrace perpetual chastity as "a transcendent sign of the Church's love for Christ, and an eschatological image of this heavenly Bride of Christ and of the life to come" (CCC 923). Like those consecrated persons who belong to secular institutes, most consecrated virgins and widows work in the world, often for dioceses or Catholic educational institutions, and while they can live alone, some choose to live in community with one another.

SELECTED READING
Pope St. John Paul II, Post-Synodal Apostolic Exhortation on the Consecrated Life and Its Mission in the Church and in the World *Vita Consecrata* (March 25, 1996), nos. 5–11

How can we not recall with gratitude to the Spirit *the many different forms of consecrated life* which he has raised up throughout history and which still exist in the Church today? They can be compared to a plant with many branches which sinks its roots into the Gospel and brings forth abundant fruit in every season of the Church's life. What an extraordinary richness! I myself, at the conclusion of the Synod, felt the need to stress this permanent element in the history of the Church: the host of founders and foundresses, of holy men and women who chose Christ by radically following the Gospel and by serving their brothers and sisters, especially the poor and the outcast. Such service is itself a sign of how the consecrated life manifests the organic unity of the commandment of love, in the inseparable link between love of God and love of neighbour.

The Synod recalled this unceasing work of the Holy Spirit, who in every age shows forth the richness of the practice of the evangelical counsels through a multiplicity of charisms. In this way too he makes ever present in the Church and in the world, in time and space, the mystery of Christ.

The Synod Fathers from the Eastern Catholic Churches and the representatives of the other Churches of the East emphasized *the evangelical values of monastic life,* which appeared at the dawn of Christianity and which still flourishes in their territories, especially in the Orthodox Churches.

From the first centuries of the Church, men and women have felt called to imitate the Incarnate Word who took on the condition of a servant. They have sought to follow him by living in a particularly radical way, through monastic profession, the demands flowing from baptismal participation in the Paschal Mystery of his Death and Resurrection. In this way, by becoming bearers of the Cross (*staurophoroi*), they have striven to become bearers of the Spirit (*pneumatophoroi*), authentically spiritual men and women, capable of endowing history with hidden fruitfulness by unceasing praise and intercession, by spiritual counsels and works of charity. In its desire to transfigure the world and life itself in expectation of the definitive vision of God's countenance, Eastern monasticism gives pride of place to conversion, self-renunciation and compunction of heart, the quest for *hesychia* or interior peace, ceaseless prayer, fasting and vigils, spiritual combat and silence, Paschal joy in the presence of the Lord and the expectation of his definitive coming, and the oblation of self and personal possessions, lived in the holy communion of the monastery or in the solitude of the hermitage. The West too from the first centuries of the Church has practised the monastic life and has experienced a great variety of expressions of it, both cenobitic and eremetical. In its present form, inspired above all by Saint Benedict, Western monasticism is the heir of the great number of men and women who, leaving behind life in the world, sought God and dedicated themselves to him, "preferring nothing to the love of Christ." The monks of today likewise strive to *create a harmonious balance between the interior life and work* in the evangelical commitment to conversion of life, obedience and stability, and in persevering dedication to meditation on God's word (*lectio divina*), the celebration of the Liturgy and prayer. In the heart of the Church and the world, monasteries have been and continue to be eloquent signs of communion, welcoming abodes for those seeking God and the things of the spirit, schools of faith and true places of study, dialogue and culture for the building up of the life of the Church and of the earthly city itself, in expectation of the heavenly city.

It is a source of joy and hope to witness in our time a new flowering of *the ancient Order of Virgins*, known in Christian communities ever since apostolic times. Consecrated by the diocesan Bishop, these women acquire a particular link with the Church, which they are committed to serve while remaining in the world. Either alone or in association with others, they constitute *a special eschatological image of the Heavenly Bride and of the life to come,* when the Church will at last fully live her love for Christ the Bridegroom.

Men and women hermits, belonging to ancient orders or new institutes, or being directly dependent on the Bishop, bear witness to the passing nature of the present age by their inward and outward separation from the world. By fasting and penance, they show that man does not live by bread alone but by the word of God (cf. Mt 4:4). Such a life "in the desert" is an invitation to their contemporaries and to the ecclesial community itself *never to lose sight of the supreme vocation,* which is to be always with the Lord. Again being practised today is the consecration of *widows,* known since apostolic times (cf. 1 Tim 5:5, 9–10; 1 Cor 7:8), as well as the consecration of widowers. These women and men, through a vow of perpetual chastity as a sign of the kingdom of God, consecrate their state of life in order to devote themselves to prayer and the service of the Church.

Institutes completely devoted to contemplation, composed of either women or men, are for the Church a reason for pride and a source of heavenly graces. By their lives and mission, the members of these Institutes imitate Christ in his prayer on the mountain, bear witness to God's lordship over history and anticipate the glory which is to come.

In solitude and silence, by listening to the word of God, participating in divine worship, personal asceticism, prayer, mortification and the communion of fraternal love, they direct the whole of their lives and all their activities to the contemplation of God. In this way they offer the ecclesial community a singular testimony of the Church's love for her Lord, and they contribute, with hidden apostolic fruitfulness, to the growth of the People of God. Thus there is good reason to hope that the different forms of contemplative life will experience *continued growth in the younger Churches* as an evident sign that the Gospel has taken firm root, especially in those areas of the world where other religions predominate. This will make it possible to bear witness to the vitality of the traditions of Christian asceticism and mysticism and will contribute to interreligious dialogue.

The West has also known, down the centuries, a variety of other expressions of religious life, in which countless persons, renouncing the world, have consecrated themselves to God through the public profession of the evangelical counsels in accordance with a specific charism and in a stable form of common life, *for the sake of carrying out different forms of apostolic service to the People of God*. Thus there arose the different families of Canons Regular, the Mendicant Orders, the Clerics Regular and in general the Religious Congregations of men and women devoted to apostolic and missionary activity and to the many different works inspired by Christian charity.

This is a splendid and varied testimony, reflecting the multiplicity of gifts bestowed by God on founders and foundresses who, in openness to the working of the Holy Spirit, successfully interpreted the signs of the times and responded wisely to new needs. Following in their footsteps, many other people have sought by word and deed to embody the Gospel in their own lives, bringing anew to their own times the living presence of Jesus, the Consecrated One *par excellence*, the One sent by the Father. In every age consecrated men and women must continue to be images of Christ the Lord, fostering through prayer a profound communion of mind with him (cf. Phil 2:5–11), so that their whole lives may be penetrated by an apostolic spirit and their apostolic work with contemplation.

The Holy Spirit, who wondrously fashions the variety of charisms, has given rise in our time to *new expressions of consecrated life*, which appear as a providential response to the new needs encountered by the Church today as she carries out her mission in the world.

One thinks in the first place of members of *Secular Institutes* seeking to *live out their consecration to God in the world* through the profession of the evangelical counsels in the midst of temporal realities; they wish in this way to be a leaven of wisdom and a witness of grace within cultural, economic and political life. Through their own specific blending of presence in the world and consecration, they seek *to make present in society the newness and power of Christ's Kingdom,* striving to transfigure the world from within by the power of the Beatitudes. In this way, while they belong completely to God and are thus fully consecrated to his service, their activity in the ordinary life of the world contributes, by the power of the Spirit, to shedding the light of the Gospel on temporal realities. Secular Institutes, each in accordance with its specific nature, thus help to ensure that the Church has an effective presence in society. A valuable role is also played by *Clerical Secular Institutes,* in which priests who belong to the diocesan clergy, even when some of them are recognized as being incardinated in the Institute, consecrate themselves to Christ through the practice of the evangelical counsels in accordance with a specific charism. They discover in the spiritual riches of the Institute to which they belong great help for living more deeply the spirituality proper to the priesthood and thus they are enabled to be a leaven of communion and apostolic generosity among their fellow clergy.

Also worthy of special mention are *Societies of Apostolic Life* or of common life, composed of men or women. These pursue, each in its own particular way, a specific apostolic or missionary end. In many of them an explicit commitment to the evangelical counsels is made through sacred bonds officially recognized by the Church. Even in this case, however, the specific nature of their consecration distinguishes them from Religious Institutes and Secular Institutes. The specific identity of this form of life is to be preserved and promoted; in recent centuries it has produced many fruits of holiness and of the apostolate, especially in the field of charity and in the spread of the Gospel in the Missions.

QUESTIONS FOR REVIEW

1. What are the three evangelical counsels?
2. What virtue do the evangelical counsels strengthen in us?
3. What does the Church call men and women living the monastic life? What about men and women living the active religious life?
4. What forms of consecrated life are devoted primarily to prayer and contemplation?
5. What forms of consecrated life are devoted primarily to apostolic work in the world?

QUESTIONS FOR DISCUSSION

1. How can life in the world sometimes distract us from pursuing Christ?
2. What advantages do you think consecrated life offers?
3. Have you ever known a consecrated person? If so, how did their witness affect you?

Chapter 2

PREPARING FOR THE CONSECRATED VOCATION

Like marriage and Holy Orders, preparation for the consecrated vocation begins long before the profession of vows. God can only call those who are listening to him, so developing a regular habit of prayer—spending time both speaking and listening to God—is essential. So is the regular reception of the sacraments of Confession and the Eucharist, both of which help us grow closer and stay closer to God. Maturing in the virtues, especially chastity, is also an essential help.

Before a person begins active discernment of religious life, there's nothing wrong with dating. It actually can be a helpful way of thinking through questions of discernment and what entering into the consecrated vocation demands of a person. Healthy, chaste relationships and friendships with members of the opposite sex, as with all the vocations, can help us grow as persons and give us insight into the path to which God calls us. Once a person has decided to discern the consecrated vocation more intensely, either with a religious order or with the help of a spiritual director, it's usually advisable to step back from dating relationships, both so that relationship doesn't confuse one's judgment and to protect the heart of the other person involved.

As a person moves forward in the discernment process, it can be a good idea to visit many different religious orders or societies, and even stay with them for a few days. This helps one become familiar with the different charisms of various orders and find a community that feels like a right fit. If a person suspects God may be calling them to consecrated virginity or a secular institute, spending time with people pursuing the consecrated vocation in those ways is similarly helpful.

Once a path is chosen, a period of discernment not dissimilar to dating begins. If a person believes God is calling them to religious life, they apply to join a particular order. If the order also discerns that God may be calling this person to their order, the person will go to live with the order and follow their way of life. This period of initial discernment is often called the postulancy and can last anywhere from six months to several years. Once the postulant determines to move forward, they enter the novitiate—a one-year (or sometimes two-year) period devoted to deeper prayer and exploration of both what the vows of religious life require and the community's life and charism. During the novitiate, novices are addressed as "Sister" or "Brother."

At the end of the novitiate, temporary vows are professed. These are usually binding for between one and four years. During this period, the religious brother or sister is fully immersed in the life of the community and engages in their apostolic work with the other members of the order.

For religious sisters, once at least three years (but generally no more than nine years) have passed, perpetual vows are professed. For religious orders, these vows are binding for life. For some societies of apostolic life (like the Daughters of Charity), vows are professed every year.

For religious brothers, the end of the novitiate is often followed by a post-novitiate period, during which time they continue both their service with the order and their formation, either for the permanent brotherhood or the priesthood. After a period of time, perpetual vows are professed and then often renewed annually.

Those who think God might be calling them to consecrated virginity or widowhood enter into a period of discernment under the guidance of their bishop. Over a period of (usually) several years, the bishop discerns that the woman is mature enough in her faith and committed to a life of chastity, poverty, and obedience to take on the vows. Retreats, spiritual reading, prayer, and spiritual direction all aid the woman in her discernment process.

discernment process [handwritten marginal annotation]

Secular institutes walk with those interested in living the consecrated vocation with them and have their own discernment process to
help people determine if this is the path God has set for them.

Unlike Holy Matrimony and Holy Orders, the consecrated vocation is not a sacrament, so the ceremonies for profession of vows differ
depending on the particular form of consecrated life the person is assuming or the order they are joining. All professions take place within the
context of the Mass and are solemn occasions filled with rejoicing and
the outpouring of special graces. Those graces may be different from the
graces of the other vocations, but they are no less helpful for the person
seeking to give themselves exclusively to God.

SELECTED READING
Pope St. John Paul II, Post-Synodal Apostolic Exhortation
on the Consecrated Life and Its Mission in the Church and
in the World *Vita Consecrata* (March 25, 1996), nos. 64–65

The mission of the consecrated life, as well as the vitality of Institutes, undoubtedly depend on the faithful commitment with which
consecrated persons respond to their vocation. But they have a
future to the extent that *still other men and women generously welcome
the Lord's call.* The problem of vocations is a real challenge which
directly concerns the various Institutes but also involves the whole
Church. Great spiritual and material energies are being expended in
the sphere of vocational promotion, but the results do not always
match expectations and efforts. Thus, while vocations to the consecrated life are flourishing in the young Churches and in those which
suffered persecution at the hands of totalitarian regimes, they are
lacking in countries traditionally rich in vocations, including vocations for the missions.

This difficult situation puts consecrated persons to the test.
Sometimes they ask themselves: Have we perhaps lost the capacity
to attract new vocations? They must have confidence in the Lord
Jesus, who continues to call men and women to follow him. They

must entrust themselves to the Holy Spirit, who inspires and bestows the charisms of the consecrated life. Therefore, while we rejoice in the action of the Spirit, who rejuvenates the Bride of Christ by enabling the consecrated life to flourish in many nations, we must also pray unceasingly to the Lord of the harvest, that he will send workers to his Church in order to meet the needs of the new evangelization (cf. Mt 9:37–38). Besides promoting prayer for vocations, it is essential to act, by means of explicit presentation and appropriate catechesis, with a view to encouraging in those called to the consecrated life that free, willing and generous response which carries into effect the grace of vocation. The invitation of Jesus, "Come and see" (Jn 1:39), is *the golden rule* of pastoral work for promoting vocations, even today. Following the example of founders and foundresses, this work aims at presenting *the attraction of the person of the Lord Jesus* and the beauty of the total gift of self for the sake of the Gospel. A primary responsibility of all consecrated men and women is therefore to propose with courage, by word and example, the ideal of the following of Christ, and then to support the response to the Spirit's action in the heart of those who are called. After the enthusiasm of the first meeting with Christ, there comes the constant struggle of everyday life, a struggle which turns a vocation into a tale of friendship with the Lord. In view of this, the pastoral work of promoting vocations should make use of suitable help, such as *spiritual direction*, in order to nourish that personal response of love of the Lord which is the necessary condition for becoming disciples and apostles of his Kingdom. Moreover, if the flourishing of vocations evident in some parts of the world justifies optimism and hope, the lack of them in other areas must not lead either to discouragement or to the temptation to practise lax and unwise recruitment. The task of promoting vocations should increasingly express *a joint commitment of the whole Church*. It calls for the active collaboration of pastors, religious, families and teachers, as required in something which forms an integral part of the overall pastoral plan of every particular Church. In every Diocese there should be this *common endeavour*, which coordinates and promotes the efforts of everyone, not jeopardizing, but rather supporting, the vocational activity of each Institute. The effective cooperation of the whole People of God, with the support of Providence, cannot but give rise to an abundance of divine gifts. Christian solidarity should abound in meeting the needs of vocational formation in countries which are economically poorer. The recruitment of vocations in these countries should be carried out by the various Institutes in full accord with the Churches of the region, and on the basis of an active and long-term involvement in their pastoral life. The most authentic way to support the Spirit's action is for Institutes to invest their best resources generously in vocational work, especially by their serious involvement in working with youth.

The Synod Assembly paid special attention to the *formation* of those who wish to consecrate themselves to the Lord, and recognized its decisive importance. The *primary objective* of the formation process is to prepare people for the total consecration of themselves to God in the following of Christ, at the service of the Church's mission. To say "yes" to the Lord's call by taking personal responsibility for maturing in one's vocation is the inescapable duty of all who have been called. One's whole life must be open to the action of the Holy Spirit, travelling the road of formation with generosity, and accepting in faith the means of grace offered by the Lord and the Church. Formation should therefore have a profound effect on individuals, so that their every attitude and action, at important moments as well as in the ordinary events of life, will show that they belong completely and joyfully to God. Since the very purpose of consecrated life is conformity to the Lord Jesus in his *total self-giving*, this must also be the principal objective of formation. Formation is a path of gradual identification with the attitude of Christ towards the Father. If this is the purpose of the consecrated life, the manner of preparing for it should include and express *the character of wholeness*. Formation should involve the whole person, in every aspect of the personality, in behaviour and intentions. Precisely because it aims at the transformation of the whole person, it is clear that *the commitment to formation* never ends. Indeed, at every stage of life,

[handwritten margin note: Why does JPII say that formation should involve the whole person?]

133

consecrated persons must be offered opportunities to grow in their commitment to the charism and mission of their Institute. For formation to be complete, it must include every aspect of Christian life. It must therefore provide a human, cultural, spiritual and pastoral preparation which pays special attention to the harmonious integration of all its various aspects. Sufficient time should be reserved for initial formation, understood as a process of development which passes through every stage of personal maturity—from the psychological and spiritual to the theological and pastoral. In the case of those studying for the priesthood, this initial formation coincides with and fits well into a specific course of studies, as part of a broader formation programme.

QUESTIONS FOR REVIEW

1. What are two things people can do to prepare themselves for consecrated life while they initially discern their vocation?
2. In a religious order, what is a postulant?
3. In a religious order, what is the novitiate period?
4. What are the two types of vows most consecrated persons make?
5. Is the consecrated life considered a sacrament?

QUESTIONS FOR DISCUSSION

1. Have you ever thought about a vocation to the consecrated life? Why or why not?
2. What do you think are some of the attractions to the consecrated life?
3. What in our culture might make it difficult for a person to want to give themselves to God in this way?

Chapter 3

CONFORMED TO CHRIST

Over the past two thousand years, countless holy men and women have fruitfully lived the consecrated vocation, giving all those called to it a model to follow in their own vocation. Of course, the ultimate model of the consecrated vocation is Jesus Christ himself. From all eternity, God the Father, the source of all holiness, consecrated God the Son for a singular mission: to redeem the world, opening for humanity the gates to heaven once more.

In time, Jesus accepted his mission from the Father, and, as Pope St. John Paul II writes in *Vita Consecrata*, consecrated "himself to the Father for the sake of humanity," embracing virginity, obedience, and poverty in "complete filial acceptance of the Father's plan."[1] Through Jesus' example, we see just how fruitful virginity, detachment from earthly goods, and obedience can be. His detachment from marriage, wealth, and even his own will freed him to do the will of the Father. As St. Paul wrote, Jesus "emptied himself, taking the form of a servant . . . and became obedient unto death, even death on a cross" (Phil 2:7–8).

Because of this, John Paul II explained:

---

[1]   Pope John Paul II, Post-Synodal Apostolic Exhortation on the Consecrated Life and Its Mission in the Church and in the World *Vita Consecrata* (March 25, 1996), §22 (hereafter cited as VC).

The consecrated life truly constitutes *a living memorial of Jesus' way of living and acting* as the Incarnate Word in relation to the Father and in relation to the brethren. It is a living tradition of the Saviour's life and message.[2]

The Paschal Dimension of Consecrated Life

Because Jesus is the exemplar of the consecrated life, consecrated persons are called to imitate him not only in his chastity, poverty, and obedience but also in his offering of himself. There is always a paschal dimension to the consecrated life. Sometimes, this is literally true, with consecrated men and women taking on the cross of persecution and martyrdom for the sake of the kingdom of God. During World War II, one consecrated woman who did that was St. Teresa Benedicta of the Cross, more commonly known as St. Edith Stein.

One of the most brilliant philosophers of her age, Edith Stein was raised in a Jewish household but had only a nominal faith. As an adult, she happened across the biography of St. Teresa of Avila. That, along with the influence of other philosophers, convinced her of the truth of the Catholic Faith. Eventually, Stein determined that God was calling her to be a nun, and she joined a religious order known as the Carmelites. With the coming of Hitler, her order moved her to a convent in the Netherlands, believing that Stein, with her Jewish blood, would be safe there. Once the Nazis toppled Holland's government, however, they came for Stein. She went willingly, believing that as a woman consecrated and conformed to Christ, it was her calling, as she said before her death, to "die for our people."

Not all consecrated men and women are called to literal martyrdoms, of course. Most are called to martyrdoms of the spirit: to be mocked, misunderstood, and dismissed for their choice to give up all that the world holds dear. They also have to give up much of what they hold dear, often

---

[2] VC §22.

living a hidden life filled with daily penances and sacrifices, all the while dying to themselves so that Christ might live in them.

The beauty of this kind of life is difficult to see, even for people who love and follow Christ. As John Paul II writes:

> It is precisely on the Cross that the One who in death appears to human eyes as disfigured and without beauty, so much so that the bystanders cover their faces (cf. Is 53:2–3), fully reveals the beauty and power of God's love. Saint Augustine says: "Beautiful is God, the Word with God . . . He is beautiful in heaven, beautiful on earth; beautiful in the womb, beautiful in his parents' arms, beautiful in his miracles, beautiful in his sufferings; beautiful in inviting to life, beautiful in not worrying about death, beautiful in giving up his life and beautiful in taking it up again; he is beautiful on the Cross, beautiful in the tomb, beautiful in heaven. Listen to the song with understanding, and let not the weakness of the flesh distract your eyes from the splendour of his beauty."[3]

As St. Augustine so beautifully expressed, there is nothing and no one more beautiful than Jesus, even on the Cross. The consecrated life reflects that beauty, not in spite of the suffering it demands but because of it. Conformed to Christ in his suffering and death, the consecrated person's life also reflects the new life that comes from that suffering and death.

Witnesses to Christ in the World

In their commitment to living the evangelical counsels and to sharing in Christ's suffering, consecrated persons bear witness to Christ in the world. They also bear witness to him through their service.

During his life on earth, Jesus made himself a servant to humanity. He

---

[3] VC §24.

healed the sick, fed the hungry, cared for the lonely, counseled the confused, ate with the outcast, taught the ignorant, and preached the Gospel to all mankind. Those acts of service were part of his larger mission to redeem humanity: to help people know God, receive his love, and love him back in return. Consecrated men and women, regardless of the form their consecrated life takes, share in this mission. It is, *Vita Consecrata* tells us, *"at the very heart of every form of consecrated life"*:

> To the extent that consecrated persons live a life completely devoted to the Father (cf. Lk 2:49; Jn 4:34), held fast by Christ (cf. Jn 15:16; Gal 1:15–16) and animated by the Spirit (cf. Lk 24:49; Acts 1:8; 2:4), they cooperate effectively in the mission of the Lord Jesus (cf. Jn 20:21) and contribute in a particularly profound way to the renewal of the world.[4]

For consecrated people, living that mission starts with themselves. Like all of us, they pursue holiness in Christ through their particular vocation. From there their mission extends to the whole world. Whether they live as contemplative religious, serving the world through prayer, or as a consecrated virgin, teaching in a seminary, the work consecrated persons do is a perpetual reminder to the world of Christ, who lived as a servant among us.

Consecrated persons bear witness to Christ through more than just their service. They also bear witness to him through who they are. As they grow closer to Christ, increasing in the virtues of faith, hope, charity, justice, temperance, prudence, fortitude, and many more, they become increasingly conformed to the image of Christ. The more joyful they are, the more we see the joy of Christ. The more patient and merciful they are, the more we see the patience and mercy of Christ. The consecrated person, in effect, is like a window to Christ or, even more accurately, like a mirror, reflecting back to the world the light that comes to them from Jesus.

---

[4] VC §25.

Their witness helps the whole Church to remember that the most important thing is to serve God freely, through Christ's grace which is communicated to believers through the gift of the Spirit. Thus they proclaim to the world the peace which comes from the Father, the dedication witnessed to by the Son, and the joy which is the fruit of the Holy Spirit. Consecrated persons will be missionaries above all by continually deepening their awareness of having been called and chosen by God, to whom they must therefore direct and offer everything that they are and have, freeing themselves from the obstacles which could hinder the totality of their response. In this way they will become true signs of Christ in the world.[5]

Mary, Consecrated from the First

While he hung upon the Cross, Jesus entrusted his mother to us. "Behold, your mother," he said to the beloved disciple; and to Mary, "Behold, your son" (John 19:26–27.) With those words, Jesus gave us both a command and a promise. He commanded us to love his mother as our own, and he promised us that his mother would love us as her own. This command and promise is for all his disciples, but it has a special power in the life of the consecrated person.

> They, like John, are called to take the Blessed Virgin Mary to themselves (cf. Jn 19:27), loving her and imitating her in the radical manner which befits their vocation, and experiencing in return her special motherly love. The Blessed Virgin shares with them the love which enables them to offer their lives every day for Christ and to cooperate with him in the salvation of the world. Hence a filial relationship to Mary is the royal road to fidelity to one's vocation and a most effective help for advancing in that vocation and living it fully.[6]

---

[5] VC §25.

[6] VC §28.

To the consecrated person, Mary is mother. She also is model and guide. Chosen by God from all eternity to be the mother of the Redeemer, Mary reminds us that it is God who calls consecrated people to follow him in a special and exclusive way. Their vocation begins with his initiative. It's not a path they make for themselves. Nor is it a path that anyone can simply choose. God must issue the call and give the grace to follow the call.

At the same time, Mary also reminds the consecrated person that God doesn't force them down the path to which he calls them. Like Mary, who responded to the angel's announcement of her role in Salvation History with the words, "Let it be to me according to your word" (Luke 1:38), consecrated persons must also give their *fiat*, their "yes" to God. God offers the grace to follow him in a uniquely close way, but each person he calls must accept that grace, not just once but every day of earthly life.

Mary models that acceptance perfectly. She was conceived without sin, like Eve, but also like Eve, she still had the freedom to sin. Eve, in the Garden, chose something other than God. Mary chose God every single day of her life. She chose God throughout her childhood, then in her home in Nazareth when the angel appeared, then as a young wife and mother raising her Son, and finally, on Calvary, where she held her dead Son in her arms. Mary's yes to God was a perpetual yes. In this way,

> the Blessed Virgin teaches unconditional discipleship and diligent service. In Mary, "the temple of the Holy Spirit," all the splendour of the new creation shines forth. Consecrated life looks to her as the sublime model of consecration to the Father, union with the Son and openness to the Spirit, in the knowledge that acceptance of the "virginal and humble life" of Christ also means imitation of Mary's way of life.[7]

---

[7] VC §28.

SELECTED READING

Pope St. John Paul II, Post-Synodal Apostolic Exhortation on the Consecrated Life and Its Mission in the Church and in the World *Vita Consecrata* (March 25, 1996), nos. 32–34

Within this harmonious constellation of gifts, each of the fundamental states of life is entrusted with the task of expressing, in its own way, one or other aspect of the one mystery of Christ. While *the lay life* has a particular mission of ensuring that the Gospel message is proclaimed in the temporal sphere, in the sphere of ecclesial communion *an indispensable ministry is carried out by those in Holy Orders*, and in a special way by Bishops. The latter have the task of guiding the People of God by the teaching of the word, the administration of the sacraments and the exercise of sacred power in the service of ecclesial communion, which is an organic communion, hierarchically structured. As a way of showing forth the Church's holiness, *it is to be recognized that the consecrated life*, which mirrors Christ's own way of life, *has an objective superiority*. Precisely for this reason, it is an especially rich manifestation of Gospel values and a more complete expression of the Church's purpose, which is the sanctification of humanity. The consecrated life proclaims and in a certain way anticipates the future age, when the fullness of the Kingdom of Heaven, already present in its first fruits and in mystery, will be achieved, and when the children of the resurrection will take neither wife nor husband, but will be like the angels of God (cf. Mt 22:30). The Church has always taught the pre-eminence of perfect chastity for the sake of the Kingdom, and rightly considers it the "door" of the whole consecrated life. She also shows great esteem for the vocation to marriage, which makes spouses "witnesses to and cooperators in the fruitfulness of Holy Mother Church, who signify and share in the love with which Christ has loved his Bride and because of which he delivered himself up on her behalf." In this perspective, common to all consecrated life, there are many different but complementary paths. Men and women Religious *completely devoted to contemplation* are in a special way an image of Christ praying on the mountain.

Consecrated persons engaged in *the active life* manifest Christ "in his proclamation of the Kingdom of God to the multitudes, in his healing of the sick and the suffering, in his work of converting sinners to a better life, in his solicitude for youth and his goodness to all." Consecrated persons in *Secular Institutes* contribute in a special way to the coming of the Kingdom of God; they unite in a distinctive synthesis the value of consecration and that of being in the world. As they live their consecration in the world and from the world, "they strive to imbue everything with an evangelical spirit for the strengthening and growth of the Body of Christ." For this purpose they share in the Church's evangelizing mission through their personal witness of Christian living, their commitment to ordering temporal affairs according to God's plan, and their cooperation in service of the ecclesial community, in accordance with the secular way of life which is proper to them.

A particular duty of the consecrated life is to *remind the baptized of the fundamental values of the Gospel,* by bearing "splendid and striking testimony that the world cannot be transfigured and offered to God without the spirit of the Beatitudes." The consecrated life thus continually fosters in the People of God an awareness of the need to respond with holiness of life to the love of God poured into their hearts by the Holy Spirit (cf. Rom 5:5), by reflecting in their conduct the sacramental consecration which is brought about by God's power in Baptism, Confirmation or Holy Orders. In fact it is necessary to pass from the holiness communicated in the sacraments to the holiness of daily life. The consecrated life, by its very existence in the Church, seeks to serve the consecration of the lives of all the faithful, clergy and laity alike.

Nor must it be forgotten that consecrated persons themselves are helped by the witness of the other vocations to live fully and completely their union with the mystery of Christ and the Church in its many different dimensions. By virtue of this mutual enrichment, the mission of consecrated persons becomes more eloquent and effective: this mission is to remind their other brothers and sisters to keep their eyes fixed on the peace which is to come, and to strive for the definitive happiness found in God.

In the consecrated life, particular importance attaches to the spousal meaning, which recalls the Church's duty to be completely and exclusively devoted to her Spouse, from whom she receives every good thing. This spousal dimension, which is part of all consecrated life, has a particular meaning for women, who find therein their feminine identity and as it were discover the special genius of their relationship with the Lord.

A moving sign of this is seen in the New Testament passage which portrays Mary with the Apostles in the Upper Room, in prayerful expectation of the Holy Spirit (cf. Acts 1:13–14). We can see here a vivid image of the Church as Bride, fully attentive to her Bridegroom and ready to accept his gift. In Peter and the other Apostles there emerges above all the aspect of fruitfulness, as it is expressed in ecclesial ministry, which becomes an instrument of the Spirit for bringing new sons and daughters to birth through the preaching of the word, the celebration of the Sacraments and the giving of pastoral care. In Mary the aspect of spousal receptivity is particularly clear; it is under this aspect that the Church, through her perfect virginal life, brings divine life to fruition within herself. The consecrated life has always been seen primarily in terms of Mary—Virgin and Bride. This virginal love is the source of a particular fruitfulness which fosters the birth and growth of divine life in people's hearts. Following in the footsteps of Mary, the New Eve, consecrated persons express their spiritual fruitfulness by becoming receptive to the Word, in order to contribute to the growth of a new humanity by their unconditional dedication and their living witness. Thus the Church fully reveals her motherhood both in the communication of divine grace entrusted to Peter and in the responsible acceptance of God's gift, exemplified by Mary. God's people, for their part, find in the ordained ministry the means of salvation, and in the consecrated life the incentive to make a full and loving response through all the different forms of Christian service.

QUESTIONS FOR REVIEW

1. How did Jesus embrace the evangelical counsels?
2. Who is St. Edith Stein? In what specific way did she model her consecrated life on Jesus' life?
3. How is the service of consecrated persons in the world an imitation of Jesus?
4. What does the angel's message at the Annunciation teach us about consecrated life?
5. What does Mary's response to the angel teach us about consecrated life?

QUESTIONS FOR DISCUSSION

1. Why do you think Jesus chose to live a life of virginity and poverty? How did that help him in his ministry?
2. Is obedience difficult for you? Why or why not?
3. Have you ever felt a call from God to do a certain act of service or follow a certain path? What was your response and why?

CHALLENGES

Isn't Having the Right Vocation, Job, or Career Essential to a Person's Happiness?

It depends on what you mean by "vocation."

If you just mean job or career, then no, not at all. In this world, jobs and careers will always be a mixed bag. Sometimes you might enjoy them. Sometimes you might not enjoy them. Sometimes they might be fulfilling. Sometimes you might feel like you are wasting your time. Almost always, there will be some stress involved. Likewise, at some point or another, you will fail at your job in one way or another.

Remember, in the Garden of Eden, one of the punishments for original sin was that work became hard. In Genesis 3:17–19, God said to Adam,

> cursed is the ground because of you;
> in toil you shall eat of it all the days of your life;
> thorns and thistles it shall bring forth to you;
> and you shall eat the plants of the field.
> In the sweat of your face
> you shall eat bread
> till you return to the ground . . .

That curse doesn't just apply to farmers. It applies to all of us. Work, in this world, will always come with some measure of difficulty, and no matter how wonderful our job is, it will never, ultimately, fulfill us or make us perfectly happy. If you expect it to, you will always be disappointed.

What matters far more than what job or career you have is how you do that job. Do you see it as an opportunity to serve God and love others? Are you kind? Are you honest? Are you offering up the difficulties that inevitably come for your good and the good of others? Are you serving the common good? When you are doing all those things, then you are living out your most fundamental vocation, which is your vocation to holiness.

That's the call you need to answer, for that is the call upon which your ultimate happiness depends. God wants you to be holy more than he wants you to have any particular job. He cares about you growing in love and virtue more than he cares about you getting a promotion at work. No matter what work you find yourself doing, that work can and should be part of your journey to holiness.

If your job is helping you to become more and more the person God made you to be, then eventually you will find happiness. If your work is getting in the way of you becoming the person God made you to be, or if it's causing you to be less than virtuous, less than loving, less than honest, then no matter how exciting it might initially seem, it will ultimately make you unhappy.

But what about if you mean something else by vocation? What if you mean a call to marriage, priesthood, or consecrated life? Or simply a call to follow God? That answer is a little different. Here, what matters is that you say yes to God if he calls you to follow him in that particular way. If he invites you to the priesthood and you say yes, but something beyond your control interferes with your ordination, you have done your part. You said yes. But if he calls you to the priesthood and you say no, that could present some problems. Refusing to answer God's call, refusing grace could become a habit that could make growing in love and virtue difficult. It also could become a habit that could lead you to give the ultimate no—the no to God, heaven, and eternal life. And that is the ultimate unhappiness.

So, in short, if you want to be happy, say yes to God when he calls, whatever he calls you to. That is the ultimate secret to happiness.

Isn't the Real Measure of Success in Life the Degree of One's Financial Security and Material Comfort?

According to the world, yes. According to the world, your success in life is determined by the money in your bank account, the title on your office door, the cars in your garage, and the number of followers you have on social media.

But that also means that, according to the world, Jesus Christ was a total failure. He was poor, never married, and at the very end of his life, abandoned by all but a few of his followers. He died on the Cross, a seeming defeat to the world that was watching at the time. In the twenty centuries since, most of his closest followers have fared no better. Most have been poor. Some have even been slaves. Almost all of them have died without an Instagram follower to their name. There is no known record of a saint who also had a collection of Porsches.

But Jesus wasn't a failure. He succeeded in his mission: obedience to the Father's will and the redemption of mankind. His followers weren't failures either. They live in eternal glory, perfectly happy, perfectly fulfilled, perfectly themselves.

That is the real measure of success. All the money in the world can't buy you joy. It can't buy you peace. It can't buy you virtue. Those are the things that last. When we die, we leave everything else behind. And when the world ends, all the things we worked so hard to acquire will burn. What endures is faith, hope, and love. Those are the virtues that make us truly holy, and only those people who acquire them—ultimately—are successful, for they have succeeded at becoming what God made them to be.

To become holy, we need to say yes to the grace God offers us and walk the path he lays out for us. In the Beatitudes, Jesus explained that path to us:

> Blessed are the poor in spirit, for theirs is the kingdom of heaven.
>
> Blessed are those who mourn, for they shall be comforted.
>
> Blessed are the meek, for they shall inherit the earth.
>
> Blessed are those who hunger and thirst for righteousness, for they shall be satisfied.
>
> Blessed are the merciful, for they shall obtain mercy.
>
> Blessed are the pure in heart, for they shall see God.
>
> Blessed are the peacemakers, for they shall be called sons of God.
>
> Blessed are those who are persecuted for righteousness' sake, for theirs is the kingdom of heaven.
>
> Blessed are you when men revile you and persecute you and utter all kinds of evil against you falsely on my account. Rejoice and be glad, for your reward is great in heaven, for so men persecuted the prophets who were before you. (Matt 5:3–12)

Those are the attitudes essential for holiness. Those are the attitudes essential for true success.

Just as People Fall in Love, They Also Fall Out of Love. Isn't a Failed Marriage Just a Regular Part of Life?

Failed marriages are very much a regular part of life in our culture. But they're not supposed to be. God did not create the institution of marriage for people to fail at it. Marriages, according to God's design, are supposed to endure "until death do us part." They are meant to be a sign of God's enduring love for us and for the Church. They are meant to teach us about the glorious, eternal communion of love within the Trinity. And to do that, they must last. Couples must be faithful to each other in good times and in bad. They must choose each other day after day after day.

This isn't easy. Feelings come and go. Life changes us in ways we don't always expect. People we love and trust can hurt us very much. In fact, because we love and trust them, when they hurt us, they hurt us more than anyone else. But, in Christ, we have the grace to choose love, grow in love, and forgive those we love.

Love is an emotion, but it's so much more than an emotion. It's an action. We love people not just by feeling love for them but by showing love—by speaking kindly, offering encouragement and support, speaking words of affirmation, doing the dishes, mowing the lawn, making coffee, remembering important dates and anniversaries, putting the laundry away, taking time to listen to the other, and a million other small acts.

We also show it by choosing to believe the best in the other, not letting a person's faults define how we see them, communicating honestly and with love, not keeping secrets, sharing in the other's joys and successes, and not letting anything else in this world—a job, a friendship, a hobby, another person—come before our marriage.

Above all, we show our love by remaining faithful to the vows we made on our wedding day: never committing adultery, never flirting or becoming emotionally entangled with anyone besides our spouse, standing by our spouse's side in good times and bad, caring for them in sickness and health, joyfully welcoming children as they come, and growing together, as a family, in faith before the Lord, drawing upon all the graces that are there for us in the sacraments.

If you do that, failure doesn't need to be a part of your marriage. Will your feelings change from day to day? Yes. But with God's grace and help your marriage will not only endure but also grow stronger and more loving with each passing year.

Don't Men and Women Who Promise Celibacy or Lifelong Chastity Live Lonely, Unhappy Lives?

The short answer? Yes. *Some* men in Holy Orders and men and women in consecrated life live lonely, unhappy lives. So too, though, do *some* married people. Some people in general live lonely, unhappy lives. Sex really doesn't have anything to do with it. It's about the person and their own emotional and spiritual struggles, the health of their relationships, and the strength of their relationship with God, not about what does or doesn't happen in their bedroom.

If continence were truly an obstacle to happiness, Jesus wouldn't have been happy. The Virgin Mary and St. Joseph wouldn't have been happy. St. Paul and the millions of men and women who have given themselves exclusively to God over the past two millennia wouldn't have been happy. But they were. Most celibates live joyful, meaningful lives, enjoying strong friendships with their brother priests or fellow religious, as well as their own families and friends who live in the world.

These men and women attest with their lives to the joy and purpose that can be found when a person lives their life exclusively for the Lord. Are there struggles? Yes. Are there sacrifices? Of course. But are there also so many graces and consolations that come when one is living continence for the sake of the kingdom of heaven, making one's entire life a gift for others? Most definitely!

There is nothing we can give to the Lord that he can't return to us tenfold. As Jesus said:

> Truly, I say to you, there is no one who has left house or brothers or sisters or mother or father or children or lands, for my sake and for the gospel, who will not receive a hundredfold now in this time, houses and brothers and sisters and mothers and children and lands, with persecutions, and in the age to come eternal life. (Mark 10:29–30)

The heart of the celibate life isn't a lack of love, companionship, or intimacy. The heart of the celibate life is an abundance of time and love and communion with Jesus Christ. And that abundance more than makes up for whatever else is lacking, giving graces that help celibate people pour out their lives even more generously for others.